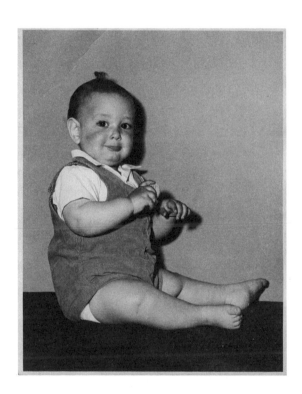

GROWING UP UNDERGROUND

A *Memoir* OF
COUNTERCULTURE
NEW YORK

STEVEN HELLER

PRINCETON ARCHITECTURAL PRESS · NEW YORK

PUBLISHED BY
Princeton Architectural Press
70 West 36th Street
New York, NY 10018
www.papress.com

Printed and bound in China
25 24 23 22 4 3 2 1 First edition

EDITOR: Jennifer Thompson
DESIGN: Matt Smith/Louise Fili Ltd
TYPESETTING: PA Press

Library of Congress
Cataloging-in-Publication Data
—
Names: Heller, Steven, author.
Title: Growing up underground : a memoir /
   Steven Heller.
Description: New York : Princeton Architectural
   Press, [2021] | Summary: "Award-winning
   designer and writer Steven Heller comes
   of age at the center of New York's youth
   culture in the mid-1960s to the mid-1970s" —
   Provided by publisher.
Identifiers: LCCN 2021059567 (print) | LCCN
   2021059568 (ebook) | ISBN 9781648960567
   (paperback) | ISBN 9781648960567 (ebook)
Subjects: LCSH: Heller, Steven. | Commercial
   artists—United States—Biography. |
   Authors—United States—Biography. |
   New York (N.Y.)—Social life and customs—
   20th century.
Classification: LCC NC999.4.H45 A2 2021
   (print) | LCC NC999.4.H45 (ebook) | DDC
   741.6092 [B]—dc23/eng/20220208 LC record
   available at https://lccn.loc.gov/2021059567
   LC ebook record available at https://lccn.loc.
   gov/2021059568

Images on pages 33, 211, 212, 216, 217, 218, 219, 220 © 2022 The New York Times Company /
All work by Brad Holland courtesy Brad Holland / Image on page 59: Alamy Stock Photos
Previous pages: 1. Cute at twelve months. Photographer unknown.
2. First drag at three. Photographer unknown. 3. Striking a pose at eighteen.
Photographer unknown. 4. Cock of the walk at eighteen. Photographer unknown.

CONTENTS

Dedicated to the people who mean the most to me
Louise Fili & Nicolas Heller

Identification cards for the School of Visual Arts,
circa September 1970 and December 1970.

PRONOUNS: ME/ME/ME

This book is about, you guessed it, me. However, it is not a trek through the hills and valleys of my autobiographical topology. I focus instead on how blind luck put me in intriguing places with curious people when, from the mid-1960s to the mid-1970s, between ages sixteen to my mid-twenties, as an art director, graphic designer, cartoonist, and writer, I was sometimes on the fringes and sometimes in the center of New York's youth culture—the alternative-sex-drugs-and-rock-'n'-roll-socially-politically-active generation, aka the boomer generation.

That said, there are a few questions that need addressing regarding my bona fides. For instance, if you can remember the sixties, were you really there? Well, how can I really be taken seriously as a counterculturist if I can vividly remember those years? Easy! I was conscious. I never experimented with psychedelic drugs or narcotics of any kind, not even a minute toke of grass (I got plenty of contact highs, though). Over-the-counter caffeinated NoDoz and St. Joseph Aspirin for Children were my uppers and downers of choice. The only mind-altering chemical I allowed in my body was helium from a tank delivered to my door on a hand truck by the *High Times* "Laff Brigade" (as a group of the editors called themselves).

I never smoked cigarettes after my mother allowed me to puff on one of her Kents when I was five (presumably to teach me an avoidance lesson). As far as stimulants go, I drank alcohol for a very short period until I ran down MacDougal Street in Greenwich Village on a bitter cold February evening with my pants off and realized I couldn't handle it.

Musically, I listened to show tunes. My pop tastes were limited to the Beatles, the Beach Boys, the Byrds, and folk-rock in general. I never liked Donovan's "Sunshine Superman" or "Mellow Yellow" (quite rightly), and, sorry, I couldn't stomach most of the Grateful Dead's repertoire and still cannot listen to their records, except for "Uncle John's Band." As the art director of the tabloid *Rock* (a *Rolling Stone* never-be), I designed some concert graphics for hard rock/psychedelic bands like Grand Funk Railroad and Blue Cheer but couldn't be bothered to listen to their albums. As for my generation's rite of passage, Woodstock, I was arrested by NYPD vice squad detectives minutes before leaving New York City for Max Yasgur's farm, thus missing that once-in-a-lifetime bragging right.

Oh yeah, sexual orientation? Straight as a ramrod. Although I lost my virginity in my early teens, it was more or less through an act of God. My nascent sex life was otherwise on the pathetic scale despite opportunities to the contrary. That arrest I mentioned above was as the "underage" co-publisher of the *New York Review of Sex & Politics.* (I was involved with other underground sex tabloids, too, which I will describe later.) "Precocious" was a word frequently used to describe me, but in truth I was painfully naïve.

For this book I've decided to relate memories that are entertaining or enlightening—or both. At least the few friends who've already heard one or more of these stories have told me they are—unless, of course, they are being polite. I had considered postponing writing this for five or ten more years, believing that the delay might stir up more page-turning content. Yet I think at my age the only stirring I'll be doing is a teaspoon of Metamucil in orange juice twice daily.

I started binge-reading dystopian novels after Donald J. Trump won the 2016 election, as if the future wasn't bleak enough. This had an unintended consequence. I came to relish George Orwell and reread the classics *1984* and *Animal Farm*, as well as *Homage to Catalonia*, his searing memoir about the Spanish Civil War. Included in my orgy of Orwellian delights was his 1946 essay "Why I Write," which I read for the first time and which inspired me. I am not making comparisons between the great Orwell and myself, other than we both write in English (well, I try to). Yet I relate to virtually every word he wrote in "Why I Write" and have no compunction about borrowing entire passages from him when I am unable to phrase my own thoughts well enough. Take this statement:

> [I] take a pleasure in solid objects and scraps of useless information. It is no use trying to suppress that side of myself. The job is to reconcile my ingrained likes and dislikes with the essentially public, non-individual activities that this age forces on all of us.

Drawing pictures was once my daily ritual. Now writing is. I write for four or more hours daily about a range of weighty and frivolous subjects for my blog, *The Daily Heller*. I have a goal in mind that is also best expressed by Orwell:

> What I have most wanted to do throughout the past ten years is to make political writing into an art. My starting point is always a feeling of partisanship, a sense of injustice. When I sit down to write a book, I do not say to myself, "I am going to produce a work of art." I write it because there is some lie that I want to expose, some fact to which I want to draw attention, and my initial concern is to get a hearing.

I wish I could accomplish a similar ambition with Orwellian passion and eloquence. I'm afraid I lack the same acuity.

I was an English major at New York University (NYU), one of two colleges (the other was Pratt Institute) out of the eight I applied to that accepted me as a freshman in 1968. I went to classes when they weren't closed down by Students for a Democratic Society (SDS), but never really buckled down. Instead, I worked happily making cartoons and comics for a few New York underground newspapers, the *New York Free Press* (the *Freep*), *Screw: The Sex Review*, *New York Avatar*, and the *Rat*. It was in these publications that I stitched together writing and drawing into one practice. To be honest, I was a third-rate Jules Feiffer, the first-rate humorist, satirist, cartoonist, playwright, and novelist whose twenty-five-year anthology I helped to edit in 1982.

That said, I did publish a comic strip in the first issue of *Screw* (in 1968 I became its founding art director). It received some notoriety at NYU

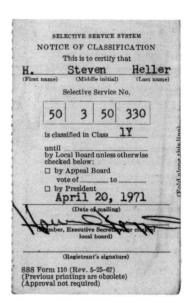

Draft cards: while enrolled at NYU, in March 1969, I was classified as II-S (student deferment); in April 1971, after I left the School of Visual Arts, I received a I-Y (temporary medical deferment).

because I used my freshman philosophy professor's name in the strip. Professor Glickman paired with his buddy Saint Anselm, who developed the ontological rationale for the existence of God, were the antiheroic duo in my mildly obscene, puerile gag, best left undescribed. The comic came to the attention of the administration—I am not sure how—and I was remanded to the university's clinical psychologist, who threatened me with expulsion if I did not submit to weekly one-on-one therapy sessions to address the root cause of my cartoon's perversity. I wasn't interested.

I refused the free counseling and accepted the consequences, forfeiting my II-S student deferment from the draft. The prospect of being sent to the Vietnam War put me in a panic. From NYU I transferred to the School of Visual Arts (SVA) illustration and cartoon program. As a white, middle-class kid living on the liberal isle of Manhattan, where so many poor African American and Latino kids voluntarily enlisted, I reported to a draft board with a very low quota to fill, and my deferment was immediately reinstated. White privilege writ large. At SVA, despite the efforts of teachers like Harvey Kurtzman—the founder of *Mad*, *Help*, and *Trump* satirical magazines—I was still a defiantly mediocre student and lackluster artist with some occasionally brilliant editorial ideas, which kept me afloat.

SELECTIVE SERVICE SYSTEM

STUDENT CERTIFICATE

(Complete Appropriate Item or Items)

1. **Name and Current Mailing Address of Student**

   H. Steven Heller
   610 East 20th Street
   New York, New York 10009

   Date January 1971

   Selective Service No.

   | 50 | 500 | 330 |

2. The student identified above has been accepted for admission for a full-time course of instruction at the college, university or similar institution of learning shown below which will commence on or about _____ .

   (Date)

3. The student identified above has entered upon and is satisfactorily pursuing a full-time course of instruction at the college, university, or similar institution of learning shown below in the ☐1st ☐2nd ☐3rd ☐4th ☐5th year class, which commenced on _____ and is expected to receive a degree on

   (Date)

   or about_____ .

   (Date)

4. The student identified above completed his ☐1st ☐2nd ☐3rd ☐4th year class on _____

   at a college, university, or similar institution of learning

   (Date)

5. The student identified above is (check one)   ☐No longer enrolled

   ☐ Not eligible to continue   ☒Graduated_____

   (Date)

6. **Remarks**

   STUDENT INTERRUPTED

INSTRUCTIONS

Selective Service Regulations define a student's academic year as the twelve month period following the beginning of his course of study.

This form may be submitted when an individual has been accepted for admission as an undergraduate student in a college, university, or similar institution of learning (Item 2) and will be submitted promptly (1) at the beginning of the student's academic year (Item 3, or Items 3 and 4) or (2) when a student is no longer enrolled, is not eligible to continue, or has graduated (Item 5). When graduation occurs, the date of graduation should be entered in the space following that caption. The original may be forwarded to the State Director of the State in which the institution is located, for distribution to local boards within the State, or to other State Directors of Selective Service, or direct to local boards. When the latter plan is followed the address of the registrant's local board should be in his possession on a Registration Certificate (SSS Form 2 or 2-A) or a Notice of Classification (SSS Form 110).

Submission of this form does not constitute a request for deferment.

Authentication of information on this form may be by any means evidencing that a responsible official of the institution has verified its preparation.

7. **ADDRESS OF LOCAL BOARD**

   Local Draft Board No. 3A
   201 Varick Street
   New York, New York 10014

8. **AUTHENTICATION**

   R. R. Hartman, Registrar

   School of Visual Arts
   209 East 23rd Street
   New York, New York 10010

   Name and address of Institution

SSS FORM 109 (REVISED 10-11-67)   (PREVIOUS PRINTINGS ARE OBSOLETE)

The January 1971 letter notifying the draft board that I was a "student interrupted" from attending the School of Visual Arts.

While I was a putative student at SVA, I worked as a cartoonist and ersatz layout artist/art director for one of the previously mentioned underground newspapers. Long story short: I preferred working at the papers every day to dutifully schlepping to boring foundation classes, like Environmental Studies. The result? Within a year I logged 90 percent absenteeism and was politely asked by the department chairperson, Marshall Arisman, to either attend my classes or leave the school. He even

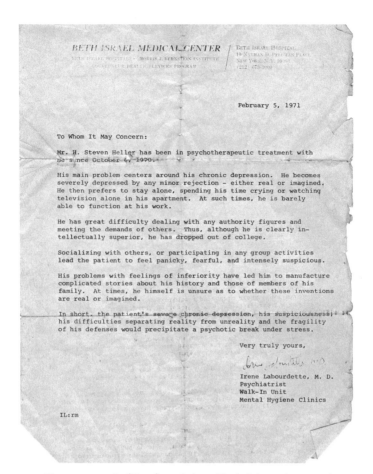

February 5, 1971

To Whom It May Concern:

Mr. H. Steven Heller has been in psychotherapeutic treatment with
me since October 6, 1970.

His main problem centers around his chronic depression. He becomes
severely depressed by any minor rejection - either real or imagined.
He then prefers to stay alone, spending his time crying or watching
television alone in his apartment. At such times, he is barely
able to function at his work.

He has great difficulty dealing with any authority figures and
meeting the demands of others. Thus, although he is clearly in-
tellectually superior, he has dropped out of college.

Socializing with others, or participating in any group activities
lead the patient to feel panicky, fearful, and intensely suspicious.

His problems with feelings of inferiority have led him to manufacture
complicated stories about his history and those of members of his
family. At times, he himself is unsure as to whether these inventions
are real or imagined.

In short, the patient's severe chronic depression, his suspiciousness,
his difficulties separating reality from unreality and the fragility
of his defenses would precipitate a psychotic break under stress.

                                    Very truly yours,

                                    Irene Labourdette, M. D.
                                    Psychiatrist
                                    Walk-In Unit
                                    Mental Hygiene Clinics

IL:rm

The exaggeratedly (I hope) worded psychiatrist's letter that earned
me I-Y status (a one-year temporary deferment from military service).
I was ultimately classified I-A, eligible for the draft.

offered to promote me straight from a freshman to a senior because of
what he referred to as the "work-study program" I was doing at my job.

Preferring to take my chances with the draft, I either opted to quit or
was officially expelled, depending on how you interpret the official record.
I managed to get a I-Y temporary health deferment for acute epiglottis,
before being quickly reclassified I-A, ripe for army induction. Yet despite
my low lottery number (fifty), I was not drafted.

Ironically, I was hired a year later to teach a newspaper design class at
SVA, and Marshall subsequently became my very close friend. I assigned
him to do some covers for *Screw*, and later, when I was hired as art director

for the *New York Times* Op-Ed page, where he was already a contributor, I continued to use him often. Eventually, I taught a class in his innovative SVA MFA/Illustration as Visual Essay program, and over time we coauthored four books about illustration. Years later, I also became friendly with Harvey and assigned him to write a story on the origin of *Mad* magazine mascot Alfred E. Neuman for the *Times* Op-Ed page. He died shortly afterward.

Thus was the bumpy yet gratifying path to becoming a self-taught, not-so-bad magazine and newspaper designer. Or as Kurt Vonnegut says in *Slaughterhouse-Five*, "And so it goes."

In 1974, at twenty-four years old, while serving a second stint as art director of *Screw* (which I had left in a huff a few years earlier), to everyone's surprise—notably my own—I was hired as the youngest art director (and occasional illustrator) for the *New York Times* Op-Ed page by the pioneering newspaper design director Louis Silverstein. I was recommended by the former *Harper's Bazaar* and, at that time, *New York Times Magazine* art director Ruth Ansel, after I showed her my *Screw* portfolio. I owe my career to her!

Over the years, the *Times* job evolved from an avocation into a profession as an expert—a historian, you might say—on the legacy of cartoons, illustrations, and graphic design. I stayed at the *Times* for thirty-three years (mostly as art director of the *Book Review*) with the inflated title of senior art director. I also wrote bylined stories about visual themes, including obituaries of designers and illustrators, in some of the *Times* feature and news sections.

I had once fantasized about being a scholar or fellow at a major university (or community college, whatever) studying tumultuous periods in political history, especially the emergence of right- and left-wing tyrannies and the hypnotic seduction of totalitarianism in pre–World War II Europe. A lack of academic follow-through thwarted that plan (I never graduated college but was awarded two honorary doctorates much later). However, I discovered a practical way of doing this scholarship thing on my own, by looking through the lens of graphic design and typographic artifacts, researching and writing on the use and abuse of propaganda. I have published a few books on these themes.

Why do I write? So that I can further discover and share what I've learned with others. I also want to validate leaving college (which I do sometimes regret). I am voraciously curious, so researching and writing have been enjoyable processes of self-education. I am fortunate to have been published in a great many outlets, including *Print* magazine, edited by Marty Fox, where I've written articles for thirty years. Currently I am a coproprietor with five partners of the online Printmag.com, which runs my eponymous (I am smitten by that lyrical word) column, *The Daily Heller*.

I compulsively publish everything I write. I hate letting anything go to waste. Around half of the published pieces are well edited by expert professionals, while the other half are barely touched by a copy editor's or grammarian's hand. What I write about is broad yet almost exclusively within the bounds of mass communication and popular culture, which includes graphic design, typography, satiric art, editorial illustration, film, and TV (I love BBC mysteries) on themes ranging from politics to technology, commerce, culture, aesthetic movements, fashion, and style. I conduct interviews for oral histories and write biographical profiles on individual artists and designers. I have authored and coauthored books, essays, interviews, articles, reviews, prefaces, forewords, introductions, and postscripts; I've done reportage, criticism, and even a couple of scripts for short video documentaries that I have narrated. Among my favorite assignments are the obituaries I write for the *New York Times*, because they combine reportage and analysis and document various individual achievements for the historical record. The subjects never complain, either. Moreover, I had a great editor, C. Claiborne Ray, who taught me a lot about structure, particularly writing compelling beginnings and snappy endings. How am I doing?

Another motivation to write is that I have trouble sleeping. I frequently used to get night terrors, which have stopped thanks to a nightly anti-demon pill. Still, I often cannot fall asleep because my mind is coursed (and cursed) with ideas for stories I want to pitch or have deadlines to write. This book is a case in point. I keep obsessing over every phrase and mull over each again and again. My ideas back up during the day, then they overflow like a clogged drain the minute my head hits the pillow. I write notes, and occasionally entire drafts, when I should be deep in REM slumberland.

I am obsessed with designed objects and graphic design as an art form that manipulates and communicates, and, as I said, design is my lens; there is always something worth examining through this camera obscura. I presume that what Orwell calls the "solid objects and scraps of useless information" that are discussed in this book will be worthy of the time it takes for you to read them. I write for myself but to serve an audience. So, I am open to comments, critiques, tips, and suggestions.

That is why I write. Now, how I write.

I start with some degree of fixation on a subject, then I free-associate based on some personal knowledge or other connection to the subject. When research is demanded, I'll take as much time as necessary to find (or hire an assistant to help find) primary, secondary, and, yes, hearsay sources. I don't fool myself that I am a trained journalist, but I've been kicking around the field long enough to use its tools.

When I think for myself and don't just regurgitate the quotes of others, I write my thoughts and craft them into a collection of satisfying sentences, paragraphs, and chapters that are usually massaged by wonderful editors. (God created editors for the likes of me.) When I have nothing original to say, I will quote or paraphrase others. Here's another Orwellian bit:

> Putting aside the need to earn a living, I think there are four great motives for writing, at any rate for writing prose. They exist in different degrees in every writer, and in any one writer the proportions will vary from time to time, according to the atmosphere in which he is living.

> (i) Sheer egoism. Desire to seem clever, to be talked about, to be remembered after death, to get your own back on the grown-ups who snubbed you in childhood, etc., etc.

> (ii) Aesthetic enthusiasm. Perception of beauty in the external world, or, on the other hand, in words and their right arrangement.

> (iii) Historical impulse. Desire to see things as they are, to find out true facts and store them up for the use of posterity.

> (iv) Political purpose. Using the word "political" in the widest possible sense. Desire to push the world in a certain direction, to alter other peoples' idea of the kind of society that they should strive after.

I agree and I subscribe to these. Obviously, if I could say it any better, I would have done so. But often others say what I'd like to say with more flair. So, thanks, George! I owe you!

A cover influenced by Aubrey Beardsley for *My Discarded Tissue*, a photocopied "literary" zine published with friends from Walden School, April 1967.

HOW TO READ THIS BOOK

've been writing, rewriting, cutting, and pasting snippets of my autobiography on and off for almost twenty years, hoping I had something
to say that was worth saying. If it is a little rough around the edges,
then I'll mention that I never formally attended classes or workshops
on memoir writing. My education comes from reading George Orwell,
Philip Roth, Tobias Wolfe, Mary Karr, Robert A. Caro, E. B. White, and
Stephen King on writing. I love reading Jill Lepore, because I admire how
smartly she balances themes from the histories of alphabets and syllabaries
to Wonder Woman.

I am on a slippery slope, uncertain about how much to reveal or
not. My manuscript is as redacted as an FBI file. I've removed or shunted
chunks of info, anecdotes, and memories for personal and legal reasons.
Indeed, my printouts are so scrawled with Sharpie expurgations, they
look like art brut. I gave up a few times, then restarted, restored, and
then stalled again, until I ultimately decided I had to shit or get off the
pot. (I'd love to know the origin of that descriptive phrase.) The turning
point came after reading (and then reviewing in *Eye* magazine) designer
Paul Sahre's splendid book *Two-Dimensional Man: A Graphic Memoir.*

I became jealous, competitive, and anxious to develop a personal voice to complete a semblance of this manuscript.

I also started pondering possible book titles. I came up with some wordplays, including *Shouts and Tremors* (because I was diagnosed with slow-moving Parkinson's disease and do love the pun on the weekly *New Yorker* humor column Shouts and Murmurs), *One Life to Live* (because as a kid I watched soap operas and this title has a nice rhythm), *I Am Not Steven Heller by Steven Heller* (the reason for which will become obvious in a subsequent chapter), and *Catcher in the Rye* (because it did so well for J. D. Salinger). I settled on the Richard Fariña–sounding *Growing Up Underground: How Sixties Youth Culture Catapulted Me into Graphic Design*, since I more or less stumbled into my artsy craft through the 1960s underground press, and this book is more or less about perpetually stumbling around during this period. Ultimately even that was simplified to the more lyrical *Growing Up Underground: A Memoir of Counterculture New York*.

This will not be a comprehensive life story. I have embroidered a sampler of essays—rather than a memoir per se—about persons, places, and things related to me and I to them and how they fit into the jigsaw puzzle of my formative years. The stories revolve around two facets of my life: the personal, which includes a psychological rationale for being a typically "rebellious" teenager, and the professional, which reveals how becoming "rebellious" led me into a career as a graphic designer and art director, starting with underground newspapers and hippie pornography and leading to the straight-and-narrow *New York Times*. So, don't be surprised (or appalled) that this is part one of two or more volumes. Where there is life there are stories.

The reader of Bob Dylan's *Chronicles: Volume One*, his unashamedly illusive memoir, never knows what's real, imagined, mistaken, or fabricated. It is Dylan's nature to be enigmatic; my nature is to tell all, when it suits me. As a Dylan fan I found his memoir captivating, especially since I personally met a few of the folks and folk singers he mentioned. Once at a party I was chatting to artist Suze Rotolo—Dylan's first New York girlfriend from the MacDougal Street folk days and a woman I had assigned to do a few illustrations for the *New York Times Book Review*—about David Hajdu's 2011 *Positively 4th Street: The Lives and Times of Joan Baez, Bob Dylan, Mimi Baez Fariña, and Richard Fariña*. She complained that his book made "an exciting time seem utterly boring." I hope that's not my destiny (although personally I liked Hajdu's book very much and was not bored at all).

I want my readers to be as interested as possible. Whatever the outcome, I promise everything that follows is like Ivory soap, at least 97 percent pure, 2 percent minor embellishment, and 1 percent memory lapse.

And speaking of Bob Dylan, I always liked the lyric from "Stuck Inside of Mobile with the Memphis Blues Again": "Oh, Mama, can this really be the end." Although, given my genetic predisposition (my parents died in their early nineties and I am seventy-one), this book will probably not be the end. I don't want to be "stuck inside" of an assisted living facility (in Memphis or anywhere else) without having attempted to record some of my life before the coil totally unravels.

The core of my story is bookended, more or less, by the mid-1960s (when the antiwar, civil rights, feminist, and hippie movements and youth, alternative, and counter cultures touched me) and the mid-1970s (when I became ensconced in the *New York Times*, cut my already receding hair, bought a few natty suits and ties, and got my first adult couch). I must also weave in some earlier contextual facts, some psychological revelations, and some asides that prevent a strict chronology that will, therefore, result in some redundancy.

So, with all that said, I'm ready to begin. Are you?

AT FILLMORE EAST January 8, 8:30 P.M

NEW YORK FREE PRESS NEW YEAR'S BENEFIT

TICKETS ARE $2.00/$3.00/$4.00/$25.00

NORMAN MAILER TALKS!!

"WHO IS THE ENEMY?"

CHARLIE MINGUS JAMS

— HIS FIRST APPEARANCE IN TWO YEARS

WITH JEREMY STEIG, DAVID AMRAM

FUGS OUTDO THEMSELVES

ED SANDERS CONDUCTS THE SHOW

CHELSEA HOTEL—222 WEST 23rd STREET

TICKETS AVAILABLE

HOUSE OF OLDIES — 267 BLEECKER ST.
NEW YORKER BOOK SHOP — 250 W. 89th ST.
DIFFERENT DRUMMER — 792 LEXINGTON AVE. (61st ST.)
CONSPIRACY — 717 LEXINGTON AVE. (59th ST.)
TAYLOR'S HOUSE OF PAPERBACK BOOKS — 2915 B'WAY (113rd ST.)

PEACE EYE BOOK STORE—147 AVE. A

TICKETS ARE $2, $3, $4 and $25
. . enclosed is $ . . . . . for . . . . . tickets
New York Free Press Benefit
200 West 72nd Street
New York City, N.Y. 10023
NAME ' ' . . . .
ADDRESS . . . .
CITY . . . .
STATE & ZIP . . . .

(Opposite) Advertisement for the *New York Free Press* benefit concert at Fillmore East, January 8, 1969. Designer: Steven Heller.

(Right) *New York Free Press*, cover, June 1968. Designer: Steven Heller.

(Bottom left) *Screw... A Sex Review*, cover, November 1968. Art director and designer: Steven Heller. Al Goldstein supplied the logo.

(Bottom right) *New York Review of Sex*, cover, April 1969. Art director: Steven Heller. Photographer: Mario Jorrin.

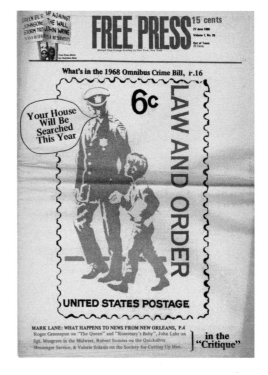

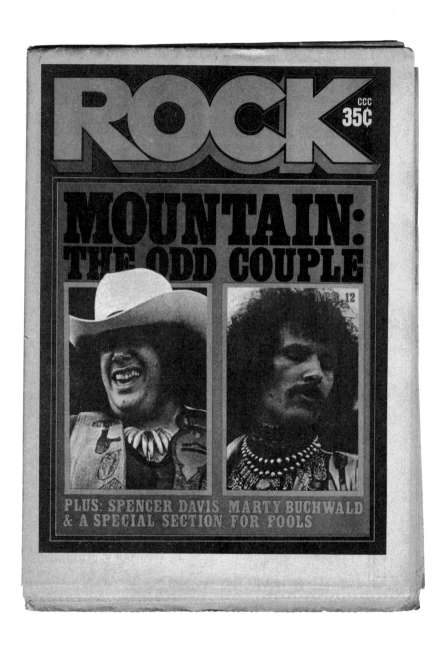

(Above) *Rock*, cover, April 1971. Art director and designer: Steven Heller.
(Opposite) *Interview: Andy Warhol's Film Magazine*, cover, July 1971. Art director:
Glenn O'Brien. Cover and logo designer: Steven Heller. Photographer unknown.

INTER/VIEW

ANDY WARHOL'S FILM MAGAZINE

JULY 1971   VOLUME II, NUMBER 4   50¢

DELL-

MURDER AS A CAREER • THE WORLD'S MOST SUCCESSFUL HOOKER
W TO START YOUR OWN RACKET • LYNDON JOHNSON: THE MAD BOM

M✪BSTER
TIMES

AUGUST/

(Opposite) *Mobster Times*, cover, August 1972. Copublisher/cover
and logo designer: Steven Heller. Vintage photograph.
(Left) *Bitch: The Only Magazine for Women*, cover, 1974.
Cover and logo designer: Steven Heller. Photographer unknown.
(Right) *Gay*, cover, January 1974. Art director and designer:
Steven Heller/World Domination Art Studio. Photographer unknown.

31

IN THIS ISSUE

A sex film without any actual sex is like a western without horses, concludes Norman Mailer, in his remarkably revealing analysis of *Last Tango* and the fundamental way in which the technique of filmmaking— improvisation vs. scripted direction— determines the life force of the film.

Dotson Rader's provocative exploration of Marlon Brando's screen persona and its relation to the American masculine mystique entitled "Death of a Stud."

The *Last Tango* reviews. Why was it necessary for so many seemingly intelligent critics to make fools of themselves? Nat Hentoff asks—and answers—the question.

Is *Last Tango* anti-woman? John Simon analyzes the charge by citing the homosexual overtones of the film and the personalities of Brando and Bertolucci.

Plus: Parker Tyler on the film's "pornography"; Judy Klemesrud interviews Maria Schneider; Dacia Maraini interviews Bernardo Bertolucci; Stuart Byron untangles Bertolucci; Charles Michener describes the "Hottest Movie." Illustrated....

(Above) E*vergreen Review,* "Closeup: *Last Tango in Paris*" (newsprint edition), back cover, 1973. Publisher: Grove Press. Designer: Steven Heller.
(Opposite) *New York Times* Op-Ed page, July 19, 1975. Illustrator: Bascove.
Art director: Steven Heller

Dangerous Case of English

By Russell Baker

The newspapers are full of mystery
ɪis week. One has the sense of
ıe reporters playing at Agatha
hristie. Profusions of clues are scat-
ered copiously through the newsprint,
o copiously, in fact, that a cautious
eader cannot help suspecting they
re not clues at all, but distractions
alculated to keep the public off the
cent of the real news.

Consider "The Case of the Out-
ooken Ambassador." At its center is
aniel Patrick Moynihan, an egghead
Irish extraction, unorthodox mind
id articulate tongue. This Moynihan
as been for years the despair of con-
entional thinkers.

Kennedyites, with whom he once
orked, were astounded when he
ossed to the Nixon White House.
acks, to whom he had once seemed
pliable white liberal, were outraged
hen he suggested that excessive
ederal promises were harmfully rais-
g black expectations the Government
ould not fulfill.

A convivial imbiber of spirit and
ape, he was sent to dwell with the
stemious Hindu and, as Ambassador

OBSERVER

New Delhi, offended Washington by
inting out that Madame Gandhi's
ar of American meddling in India
ght not be unreasonable in view of
C.I.A.'s meddlesomeness in Chile.
At length, Messrs. Ford and Kissinger
spatched him to the United Nations,
nking perhaps that live burial in
s backwater cemetery of diplomacy
ould crush his spirit and Moynihan
ould be heard of nevermore.

Alas, Moynihan spoke English, an
cient tongue which, though long
len into disuse, still has the power
sway men's minds, and upon arrival
the United Nations, he outraged all
manity by speaking it aloud.

Minute autocracies and tribal king-
ms, which wield a majority of the
N.'s votes and one-and-one-half per-
nt of its power were appalled.
ropeans were appalled. Washington
s appalled, or at least that vast part
Washington that is the State De-
rtment and Henry Kissinger.

And yet, Moynihan could not be
ed. He had spoken English in de-
se of Israel. What President, what
cretary of State dares fire an Irish-
n who has raised his shillelagh in
cause sacred to the heart of the
vish vote? And with an election
ar approaching!

The President summoned Moynihan
Washington, pronounced him his
y and sent him back to the Waldorf-
oria. A calm ensued, although
ny readers of newspaper mysteries
ected muffled sounds of dirty work
the butler's pantry. Reporters who
oy the hospitality of State Depart-
nt men and even of Kissinger began
culating publicly that Moynihan was
aking English for base and selfish
itical gain. In brief, that he was
rely trying to ingratiate himself
h the Jewish vote so as to launch
political career in New York.

One could read this two ways: (1)
was correct. (2) Somebody was
soning the well by trying to paint
ynihan as an opportunist in diplo-
's clothing. I held both possibilities
n and allowed for the fact that
re might even be a third.

Very soon, we had a personal at-
k on Moynihan's use of English by
British U.N. representative, an oc-
rence so out of character with
don's bland diplomatic style that
rned the papers back a few pages
re-read for overlooked clues. Lo
behold if Kissinger had not been
London shortly before. Not only
t. He had had a long talk with the
tish Foreign Minister. I put Kis-
ger down as a possible suspect in
plot, but still could not grasp what
plot was.

This week, a sudden outburst of
ion. The newspapers bloom with
ked reports that Moynihan is up
his old tricks. He has resorted to
glish again. This time he has writ-
a memo and circulated it all over
State Department's wire system.
accuses the State Department of
ng to undercut his attempts to
y out his assigned job at the U.N.
he newspapers play this leaked
mo as a big story, but aficionados
mystery news instantly recognize
t the papers are concealing the
st interesting part: The real ques-
is who leaked the memo and why.
it was Moynihan, which is pos-
e, was it to force a showdown with
e and Kissinger? If it was State
Kissinger, was it to force a show-
n that would at last rid them of
troublesome English speaker?
papers tell us nothing, although
t day we have the customary White
se declarations that Ford and Kis-
er stand behind Moynihan.

he day after that, however, the
ers begin to give us mysteriously
tributed reports that Kissinger
Ford can't say it aloud, but are
ally at the end of their patience
Moynihan. Scolding editorials
written deploring Moynihan's
equate diplomatic finesse. (His
t of using English.)

omething is going on here. What
s is a mystery. If the reporters
w, why do they not tell us? One
he things that is going on is ob-
s enough. The papers are letting
nselves be used by Government
ipulators in return for a story that
poor substitute for the story of
t is really going on.

Woodcuts by Bascove

A Threat to Blacks In Higher Education

By Christopher F. Edley

QUIET REVOLUTION is taking place within Congress that if successful could spell disaster for blacks in higher education.

A House of Representatives subcommittee is working on legislation to replace the Student Financial Aid Act, which expires June 30, and from every indication it involves a fundamental philosophical and practical shift away from blacks and other minorities.

The premise of Federal financial help up to now has been that universal access to higher education in America to be meaningful requires specific pointed assistance to those who need it most. The goal has been clear: to overcome the inequality of opportunity that historically has prevented young people from low-income families and disadvantaged minority groups from enjoying the benefits of higher education.

With Representative James O'Hara, chairman of the House subcommittee on post-secondary education, that goal appears to have changed. The new thinking is toward helping the middle class more substantially. No one is against such help except that Federal student aid funds are limited and there is no increase in sight. To dissipate the scarce funds over a wider target area destroys the original purpose of aiding those students with the greatest need.

Several proposals are being considered to accomplish a shift in funding priorities to favor the middle class. Mr. O'Hara has suggested the elimination of total assets other than family income in determining the financial need of applicants. Another recommendation is to lower the basic minimum grant to $100 from the previous $200 level, the theory being that you spread aid to more students that way.

The net result of spreading financial aid without a corresponding increase in the appropriation is to take funds from the hide of low-income students who need more help, not less. As any parent or student would testify, the $1,400 maximum grant is far below what a low-income student requires to attend college.

A further change being contemplated by the subcommittee calls for the addition of an academic merit criterion as a basis for student aid support. Standardized tests are already the subject of enough controversy because of the way they are inherently biased against minority students. The introduction of that kind of measurement standard would cement the disparity in access to higher education already existing between blacks and whites. The socio-economic factors that go into creation of slums and segregated ghetto schools in America are too well documented to have to be debated at this late date—or to be perpetuated by the Federal Government's getting involved in determining who is smart enough to attend college.

Blacks in this country are going to college in number as never before. In the last five years there has been a 60 percent increase in the enrollment of blacks in higher education. Black colleges, which are in the business of educating low-income students, have been increasing their enrollment at twice the rate of the total collegiate sector. Most of the entering black freshmen are a previously untapped resource for America—poor and needy kids who are the first in their families to go to college and to break the cycle of poverty that has chained them. In the last decade, hundreds of thousands of blacks from the lowest economic ranks have graduated from college with the help of these Federal aid programs, and they are now pouring millions of dollars into our economy through their taxes and spending from income.

For 25 years we have struggled to motivate blacks to attend college. Now just when it seems we have had a breakthrough, the rules are being changed. A decrease in financial aid to low-income students along with the decline of open enrollment in New York City and cutbacks in the recruitment of minority students by predominantly white schools all say that the education of the poor and disadvantaged is a low priority and that in an economic crunch they will be the first to go and the last admitted.

This is not the time to roll back progress. This is not the time to slam the door in the face of thousands of young blacks, poor whites, Mexican-Americans, Puerto Ricans and other needy youngsters.

Christopher F. Edley is executive director of the United Negro College Fund.

Equality in Britain: 'Envy' and 'Bourgeois Guilt'

By Margaret Thatcher

o WHAT EXTENT is more equality desired in Great Britain today? Statistical myths lead directly to the claim that there is a widespread sense of resentment and injustice over the current degree of inequality in our society and great enthusiasm for its elimination. This political judgment is closely linked in many commentators' eyes with the quite separate proposition that class divisions in Britain are severe and reinforced by economic inequality.

My own experience in politics has always made me doubt that argument. Now, fortunately, more work has been done.

We have had a massive survey of political and economic groups reported in July, 1975.

This is what it showed: ". . . little spontaneous demand for the redistribution of earnings across broad occupational categories and (the suggestion) that any such redistribution would in itself provide no solution to any problems of pressure-on-pay. Neither is it necessary to allay any general feelings of injustice in society. . . . It may be little consolation to the Government in present circumstances that the chief requirement for maintaining general satisfaction with incomes and earnings is steady economic growth . . . rather than massive redistribution. . . . This point is a crucial one to be met by those who suggest that any problem we have is one of distribution rather than of resources of growth."

Despite the evidence of what ordinary people actually want, there remains in Britain a powerful and vocal lobby pressing for greater equality—in some cases even, it would seem, for total equality. One tries to analyze what it is that impels them to do so.

Of course, one important pressure is undoubtedly the ordinary desire to help our fellow man. But often the reasons boil down to an undistinguished combination of envy and what might be termed "Bourgeois Guilt."

Envy is clearly at work in the case of the egalitarian who resents the gap between himself and those who are better off, while conveniently forgetting his own obligations to those poorer than himself.

Bourgeois Guilt is that well-known sense of guilt and self-criticism that affects people, not only the very rich, when looking the other way, at the position of those poorer than themselves. It is not for me as an individual to criticize or ridicule their doubts and worries. But, as a politician, I must criticize the attempts of such people to impose on others a program of impoverishment through the medium of the state. That brings happiness to no one except to those who impose it.

In a free society, they can give away as much as they want to, to whom they want to. If they believe in pooling their possessions with others in a commune, they are welcome to do so.

The point is that it has been shown that there is a far less general desire for equality, as opposed to equity, in Britain today, than is often claimed.

The facts about equality are that people don't appear to want further distribution. They are more interested in growth and new resources of wealth.

Margaret Thatcher is leader of Britain's Conservative Party. This is an excerpt from an address at a conference here on welfare reform sponsored by The Institute for Socioeconomic Studies.

An Optimistic View Of Agriculture's Future

By David P. Harmon Jr.

VER THE LAST two years, a pessimistic outlook for the future of world agriculture has arisen. This outlook has been fueled by constant repetition that ever-more-serious food shortages are to occur because of exponential population growth, rising affluence, and lack of resources and technology. The facts, however, permit a more optimistic view.

First, it is clear from the experience of Western industrialized countries, the Soviet Union, Japan, South Korea and Taiwan that population growth rates decrease with economic development. The attendant urbanization, increased incomes, literacy and improved health bring about changes in personal priorities and values that result in smaller families. Declining birth rates over the last decade in such widely divergent societies as those of China, Egypt and Costa Rica offer evidence that the demographic transition is spreading beyond the developed world.

A concomitant of economic development is rising affluence, which entails increased effective demand. The suggestion that the United States and others reduce consumption to make food and fertilizer available to developing countries ignores one very basic fact—effective demand calls forth supply. If demand is curtailed, farmers will produce less, and thus less will be available for foreign purchase and aid.

Cropland is not the limiting factor in expanding food production. The world's supply of arable land could be virtually doubled by opening large portions of Latin America and sub-Saharan Africa. More important, however, is the investment made to increase cropland's productivity by irrigation, chemical fertilizer and better farming techniques, among other means.

As a dynamic activity, agriculture, just as industry, benefits from productivity increases and cost reductions. Fertilizer, just one of many considerations, reflects this dynamism. Production costs decrease because of technological advances, economies of scale, and more efficient manufacturing techniques. Productivity increases as farmers learn to use fertilizer more effectively, and the productivity of labor, machinery and irrigation rises with more effective application.

Real United States grain prices and costs declined over the period 1910-1971 while production increased substantially. The greater output at lower costs indicates that incentives existed to create more efficient methods of production. For example, over the last 20 years, American farmers have produced one-third more wheat on one-third fewer acres.

Increasingly, man improves on nature in raising food—witness his use of high-yield-seed varieties with specific desired characteristics, his creation of single-cell protein in factories.

Innovations in food production, however, need not necessarily be exotic to be dramatic. Britain's Glasshouse Crops Research Institute recently developed the nutrient film technique, a novel yet simple method of growing crops without soil in polyethylene gulleys. This low-cost closed-environment system conserves water and fertilizer and is potentially suitable for the developing-country farmer operating under poor topographical or climatological conditions. In use today in over 20 countries, primarily for vegetables, this method may be used to grow rice and wheat at a reasonable cost in the future.

The critical factor in increasing agricultural production is a realistic and intelligent approach to institutional requirements that permits resources and technological capabilities to be fully realized. Too often, developing-country governments have discouraged agricultural progress through ill-conceived policies and inappropriate actions. Most economic-development plans prematurely emphasize heavy industry with a resulting misallocation of resources for the economy and a patchwork of policies for the agricultural sector.

Governments can play a very positive role by providing the economic and technical environment to encourage the farmer to produce. Developing-country governments can facilitate increased agricultural production by giving priority to agriculture, focusing on the individual farmer and the specific requirements of agriculture in various locations, designing technologies that help sidestep institutional barriers such as the high cost of petroleum-based materials, and enabling the private sector to perform those activities for which it is best suited while the government fills those needs that the private sector cannot.

Apocalyptic predictions about a growing world population running out of food have been proved wrong. We have many avenues for providing ample food in the future.

David P. Harmon Jr. is a member of the staff of the Hudson Institute, Croton-on-Hudson, N.Y., a research organization.

Cancer Along The Edges

By C. L. Sulzberger

BRUSSELS—The most significant recent trend in Western Europe has not been an advance toward economic and political unity after two decades of faltering along that road but the perceptible crumbling along the edges of the NATO alliance without which European safety and prosperity cannot long endure.

The periphery of the coalition is rusting away. Iceland (whose geographical facilities are essential to Atlantic protection) and Britain are again scrapping over codfish.

Portugal is waiting to see if it can survive without Communists in key positions. The status of Italy as an ally depends on whether it can compose a government. And Greece and Turkey, so obsessed by their squabble, are both weakening their NATO ties.

The only good news comes from France, which has quietly strengthened relationships with the alliance although, in order to avoid internal political recriminations, it prefers not to talk about this. And even if things have improved, Paris still holds back

FOREIGN AFFAIRS

from any form of peacetime integration with NATO's other forces.

Today some old hands are beginning to wonder if the alliance can—or, indeed, should—continue in its present form or whether it might not better return to the concept of a little NATO originally favored by several founding fathers.

The little NATO idea envisioned only a small, well-knit bloc of partners around which European defenses could be built: West Germany, France, the Benelux countries, Britain, plus a committed United States and Canada. The idea was that these nations had common interests and parallel views which would not be subordinated to regional deviations such as those to which Mediterranean or Scandinavian allies might be subjected.

A classic case in point is that of Greece and Turkey. They were admitted to NATO in 1952, although several statesmen warned that their participation would be uncertain and flawed because of their long history of disputes and their relative isolation from other partners. This has indeed proved to be the case.

Even during his first term as Prime Minister, in the 1950's and early 1960's, Constantine Caramanlis had difficulty keeping the emotional Greeks loyal to NATO because of their irritation with Turkey over Cyprus. Now, in the 1970's, Mr. Caramanlis (although personally pro-NATO) has had to bow to public pressures by partially withdrawing Greece.

■

NATO has not proved useful as a club within which disputes can be settled. Secretaries General Spaak, Stikker, Brosio and Luns have all been involved in the Greco-Turkish argument. None has been a triumphant peacemaker; nor have other NATO leaders, including American Presidents and Secretaries of State.

The closest anyone got to success was President Lyndon Johnson. At his behest Dean Acheson, a special mediator, wrote to Greece's then Prime Minister, George Papandreou, on Aug. 20, 1964: "I am prepared to apply the utmost pressure and persuasion to get the Turks to give up any claim for sovereign territory on Cyprus, to reduce the dimensions of their requirements for a military base on the Karpas Peninsula and to settle the rights of minorities along the lines which I have discussed. . . .

"I would do my best, and believe I could succeed, in obtaining the agreement of the Government of Turkey not to intervene to prevent or to demand prior intergovernmental agreement before the achievement of *enosis* between Greece and Cyprus."

This proposal was accompanied by a map showing the Karpas Peninsula, proposed as a Turkish base, comprising only a bit more than 5 percent of the area of Cyprus. But Mr. Papandreou, for reasons which appear insane in view of subsequent developments, spurned the offer at the last minute. Turkey also disdained it.

■

Athens later ignored a proposal from Mr. Johnson to Mr. Papandreou (Aug. 28, 1964) that the Karpas Peninsula be ceded to Turkey in perpetuity. Compare that proposal twelve years ago with the situation prevailing now as Bonn makes another mediation attempt for NATO's sake.

The Cyprus dispute is only one example of the kind of argument that has continually plagued the alliance because members give priority to national political interests over defense or international peace. This type of situation has existed all too long. One sometimes wonders if it is worth tolerating indefinitely.

If NATO's peripheries cannot be strengthened—perhaps helped by Spain's inclusion in the alliance—surely it is not beyond the abilities of industrial powers in the twentieth century's final quarter to devise a substitute system for their military protection, based only on the proven resolution of perhaps a smaller group of powers directly linked to the West's vital heart.

CHAPTER ONE

To Begin With...

I am not Steven Heller.

Well, to be exact, Steven Heller is not my full legal name. My parents, Bernice and Milton (typical Jewish names at the time) Heller, branded me with Harmon Steven Heller when I was born on July 7, 1950, and it remains so on my passport and tax returns, although everything else—driver's license, credit cards, employment records, MetroCard for seniors, etc.—reads Steven Heller. I never legally changed my name despite strong suggestions to do so. But we need not explore that conundrum now.

Harmon was my given name in memory of my mom's beloved father, Herman Metzger, who passed away days before I was conceived, eight years or so into my parents' sixty years of marriage. Herman never learned about the blessed news. Obviously, I never met him, and, sadly, I have only seen his countenance in a couple of colorless photos that revealed little if any family resemblance.

I heard he was a snappy dresser and a bon vivant, gregarious and ultra-philanthropic until he lost all his investments in the Great Depression. He was a stock gambler who, like millions of other believers

My grandfather Herman Metzger (date unknown).
My mother never had an opportunity to tell him she was pregnant
with me. He died of a sudden heart attack in 1949.

in capitalism, took a fatal hit when in 1929 the market crashed. His shlock stock transformed my Grandma Ray's comfy Grand Concourse lifestyle from Jewish nouveau riche to Bronx penury. Although it caused her considerable heartache, she never burdened me with the bitterness that was her right, although she admitted to having chronic anxiety (one of my own maladies, which I probably have inherited).

Herman was never able to climb out of the hole he dug for himself buying shares on margin. The lesson Grandma Ray learned was never ask for credit and you will not go into debt. In the sixties, when large banks were issuing credit cards like candy to college-aged, counterculture kids—it was like economic monetary marijuana—I signed up and immediately incurred a large, compounded debt. Fearing that I not only had a variant of Grandpa Herman's name but also inherited his gambler's gene when I was

My grandmother Ray (Zuckerbrot) Metzger, circa 1912, in New York City,
prior to meeting and marrying Herman.

eighteen, Grandma Ray generously paid off the Mastercard and Visa bills and made me promise not to use credit cards ever again. I avoided them for about a year.

Perhaps before Herman died, the knowledge of the long-awaited grandchild—me—would have given him some solace, even renewed pride, and a modicum of happiness to overcome his failure. But I'll never know; a weak heart did him in while my mom was waiting for a good moment to break the news.

There's so much I don't know about Grandpa Herman, and it is sad that we are so genetically close yet so cosmically distant. Although I sometimes asked to learn more details about him, I was never given the keys to our family closet. What I knew was that Herman was born in a region of the Austro-Hungarian Empire, Galicia, that was ceded to Poland after World War I. In any case, he landed at Ellis Island before all that geopolitical mishigas. In New York he tried out a few minor business schemes then settled on a butter-and-egg store located on the Upper East Side of Manhattan. Before the financial catastrophe, he drove an expensive American dream car and lived in a wealthy part of the Jewish Bronx with my Grandma Ray, my mom, and her younger brother, my Uncle Walter, in a splendidly appointed Grand Concourse apartment, which I hazily remember visiting as a three- or four-year-old, shortly before Grandma was forced to move to less expensive lodgings behind a once grand hotel turned welfare-housing dump. Living behind the Concourse Plaza Hotel was not totally without benefits; it was three blocks east of Yankee Stadium and a short distance from the Polo Grounds.

It is no wonder my grandma suffered from chronic anxiety. Her first-born child, my Uncle Felix, succumbed to the 1918 Spanish flu pandemic at two years old. He is buried in Brooklyn under a weathered tombstone topped, as was the custom, with a little lamb, which is now eroded almost beyond recognition. My mother was born in 1919, and then Uncle Walter in 1921; he had scarlet fever for a year.

Herman had at least one wealthy brother, Morris, who owned a successful ladies'-coat business. Morris was conservative with his investments and did not go bust in the crash. In fact, when his own children pushed him out of his business many decades later for being "too old," he collected the coat fabric remnants lying around the factory and began making a profitable line of hats.

Even though I was named for my mother's side of the family, I always believed they considered me more genetically part of my father's side of the family, which ostensibly emigrated from a shtetl in Russia by way of Vilnius, Lithuania. I don't really know much about them, though my great grandfather was Jacob Geller; in Russian "G" is pronounced as a guttural, phlegmy "H." When I was little, my father's family met once a year at a meeting room on Manhattan's Union Square to discuss the family funeral plot. The group was called the Jacob Heller Circle. I was once tempted to name an underground newspaper with that title.

My middle name, Steven, is an Anglicized way of honoring Schmuel, Grandma Ray's father, whom, my family believes, was killed in the Holocaust somewhere between Lodz and Auschwitz. The only evidence of this is a postcard from Lodz with Nazi marks rubber-stamped on it. It states in his handwriting that he and the family he left behind were okay. His name was Schmuel (or Samuel) Zuckerbrot (sugar bread), and his relatives in New York, who took in his daughter, Grandma Ray, before World War I, were the Messings. This family owned the Messing Bakery, makers of fine bread—a loaf of which my family would loyally keep in the breadbox. I do not know much more. On a visit to the Galicia Museum in Krakow and a day trip to Auschwitz, I was unable to find any trace of the Zuckerbrots. My family history is a mystery that even ancestry.com has failed to solve.

I do know, however, that my mom did not want me going through life with the name "Herman." So, the Anglicized Harmon (Irish [mainly County Louth]: generally of English origin; but sometimes also used as a variant of Harman or Hardiman, that is, an Anglicized form of Gaelic Ó hArgadáin [see Hargadon] English: variant spelling of Harman) was an acceptable alternative. It sounded more mellifluous and less Germanic than did "Herman." Yet for me, "Harmon" was just as much of an albatross. I have no idea what naming books my mom read or where she came up with it or why my father agreed to it. I just hated it from when I was old enough to pronounce it. It was a point of rebellion.

Baseball trivia fans might know that back in the 1950s there was a baseball player named Harmon Killebrew, known as Hammerin' Harmon, who played for the Washington Senators and Minnesota Twins. But my parents didn't follow baseball, so it did not derive from him. Of course, for my prepubescent years, kids, coaches, and camp counselors persisted in calling me Killebrew, which sounded even more ridiculous. "Harmon" also carried with it some annoying nicknames, such as Harm, Harmy, Harmbone, and Harmala. "Chaim Schmuel" was my liturgical Hebrew name. So, in Hebrew school I was called Chaim. Also annoying!

Another reason that the name was anathema was that there was no one else called Harmon anywhere in New York City, where I was born and raised, or in Long Beach, Long Island, where I spent summers. For that matter, no Harmons existed in any of the schools, clubs, organizations, etc. that I belonged to. Although Bob, Dave, Joe, Bill, and a host other common American names were admittedly boring, they were normal. I preferred boring to "What the fuck is a Harmon?" I'm convinced Harmon ruined my chances in various life scenarios. My wife, Louise Fili, once seriously said that she probably would not have wanted to go out with me if I were known as Harmon Heller. (I admitted my full name to her a year after we met.)

One final reason that I disliked my given name is that in elementary school, I sat next to a very smart Puerto Rican girl named Carmen Morales. We became known as Harmon and Carmen, which would have been great if we were Latin entertainers, but not so great when we were called upon by our teacher to answer a question or make a presentation. Carmen always got the answers right, while I was hit-or-miss, mostly the latter. Can you imagine how humiliating it was to say, "Yes, Mrs. Goldblatt" when the teacher was calling on Carmen and I misheard "Harmon"? It may sound insignificant, but at eight years old it made the students laugh and made me squirm.

I hated the Harmon part of me.

When I was fifteen years old, my parents went on a monthlong sight-seeing trip to Russia and sent me with a family friend, Lilly Ruglass, to stay with some of her relatives who lived north of Stockholm. I loved Sweden, not just for the beautiful blonde girls, beautiful scenery, and beautiful smoked fish, but mostly because, for some reason that I still do not entirely understand, Swedes refused to call me (or simply could not pronounce) Harmon. It was as impossible to them as "Mister Mxyzptlk" is to readers of *Superman* comics. Instead, they decided it was easier to call me Steve or Steven. Wow. I no longer had to be Harmon. I could change my name if I wanted to. The relief I felt was palpable.

I stayed in Sweden a few months, living with a few different families who not only called me Steve but also taught me to think differently about politics. It was 1966. I was fifteen. United States involvement in the Vietnam

War was in its early stages. The older members of the families I lived with were vociferously against US involvement in this war, and they spoke English well enough to tell me why. Night after night, I listened to harangues against US policy. They'd say, "Steve, don't you understand that South Vietnam is an American puppet state, just like being a French colony. And the Vietnamese should have their own right to self-determination, Steve!" The more they said "Steve," the more I listened, and the more my fourteen-year-old-having-once-gone-to-summer-school-at-Valley-Forge-Military-Academy-because-I-wanted-to-join-the-Air-Force brain was beginning to be washed clean of all its blind patriotism.

Swedish teens were going further out than Americans into the anti-establishment world. I was exposed to Swedish liberation at midnight sun concerts—this was 1966—with semipolitical rock groups like the today unknown Horselips, whose male members wore shoulder-length hair, longer than the Beatles at that moment. They were more raucous in their performance styles too—almost like punk but with a hybrid Merseybeat, blues, and rock 'n' roll aliveness. And the kids in the audience were dressed and coiffed accordingly—the guys with shaggy hair with bangs, and the girls with long, flowing, straight, parted-down-the-middle hair. They were so fucking cool, and I felt so fucking square with my short-cropped, parted-to-one-side blandness. I wanted my hair to grow long. I wanted my name to be changed forever.

A thought soon hit me—not only was I changing my name, but also I was changing my philosophical, political, and cultural points of view. Next, I would become sexually aware, but that's an embarrassingly convoluted story for another time. The first four changes were pretty heavy life shifts. My parents had sent me to live briefly in Sweden because they wanted to go on a trip. And although they had previously gone away and left me on my own or with family friends or relatives, they usually returned to the same Harmon Heller. This homecoming came as a shock to them.

Evolving into my new self would take many turns, but first my parents had to accept my transformation and start calling me by my new name. I refused to answer to anything but Steve. This was even more difficult for my poor grandparents, who would have to learn (and remember) I was no longer and would never again be Harmon, their little boychick. After all they'd been through—from starting over after leaving Vilnius, Galicia, and wherever else they lived in villages, cities, and ghettos as younger people, to losing family in Hitler's war against the Jews—they were used to major changes to and in their lives. And now here comes my indulgent conversion. For the rest of their lives, I wondered, would they be prejudiced against Sweden? Or would they be exactly what I knew them to be, loving grandparents who adored me no matter what, because that's what good grandparents do?

Returning from Sweden to New York, I was H. Steven Heller. I kept the H in deference to Herman. But I became someone else—a rebel-in-training, trying to earn my beads. Now it was time to expose myself to the world, such as it was, around me.

Hand-painted photograph of me, probably around twelve or thirteen
months old. My father often said of this photo that I reminded
him of Jackie Gleason, the rotund comedian.

CHAPTER 2

The Appointment Baby

S teve was an appointment baby," my mother blurted out. She was talking to Pat Morris, the first of my three wives. It was within the first five minutes of sitting down to the get-to-know-the-new-in-laws dinner.

"It was the thing to do," she continued, referring to a couple of "professional women colleagues" who found that the appointment option "made planning their social calendars and made being new mothers these days so much easier."

Appointment baby? What the hell was an appointment baby, anyway? Have any of you heard this term? It was new to me. Why was I an appointment baby? And what impact, if any, did it have on my early and later life?

This seems like a good place to start my story.

My mom, born Bernice Metzger, was proud of being a professional woman. A first-generation American born in 1919, she grew up during the Great Depression and went to Hunter College in New York, where she earned a BS in physical education and gymnastics. Hers was the first college degree in the Metzger family; her brother, my Uncle Walter, later got his PhD in American history. Mom was a competitive Ping-Pong champion and played basketball too. She was attractive, stylish, and very popular within the New York Jewish milieu (although she was restricted from gentile circles because she was a Bronx Jew).

Did I mention she was competitive?

In her early twenties, during World War II, my mom decided she was better suited to retail than teaching gym in New York City public schools and took jobs at clothing and department stores in Southern cities. These included Savannah, Georgia, where my dad, Milton Heller, who came from a similar but poorer immigrant Bronx Ashkenazic background and graduated from City College of New York, was stationed at an Army Air Force base as a warrant officer/accountant. They met through friends; more than that I don't know.

Eventually, my mom turned her talent for retail buying and selling into developing preteen clothing lines. She had a successful fifty-year career as a buyer for a couple of major department store parent companies. To her credit she withstood a lot of badgering and rebuking from her mother, in-laws, relatives, and even some lifelong girlfriends about being a part-time mom and how that would screw me up. It was fine for women to have jobs during the war and before bearing their children, but society frowned upon mothers who had all-consuming careers. She hated the disdain from family and friends but loved competitively lording over them the fact that she was special for following a separate life path. I think that's when her narcissism kicked in, and it grew from there as a linchpin of her life.

For me, an only child, her career had mixed consequences, including a lifelong tally of unmet psychological needs and simmering resentments that shaped my acutely neurotic but nevertheless moderately stable existence. I learned to be self-reliant, which was a plus. One other advantage I gained is that I have always been punctual for appointments—even without wearing a watch for most of my life (until the cell phone imposed a clock function, which I use on occasion).

As for my appointment birth, I arrived right on time, almost exactly as planned: 2:15 a.m. on Tuesday, July 7, 1950, at the since-demolished Beth David Hospital in Manhattan on the Lower East Side. Even the doctor was amazed by the level of precision.

But why so early in the morning if my mom had her pick of appointment dates? After some prodding, she confessed wanting to complete a full day at her job before my arrival. "I had to finish some work," she told me in all seriousness. I presume it was a matter of pride. I know it was a portent of things to come, particularly since I still rise almost precisely around 3 a.m. every morning, if only for a few minutes.

Until that particularly unsettling dinner with Pat, the term "appointment baby" had never been uttered. Apparently, it was one of the curious facts concerning my early life that was kept secret either for some ulterior reason or simply benign neglect. Who knows? Closed lips keep emotions at bay. But now that I was twenty years old and married, the appointment phenomenon quickly became a leitmotif. Whenever my mom met my friends or others I was involved with—out came the appointment story.

No big deal, right? Kind of emancipated on her part, right?

Wrong!

Appointment babyhood was born out of a neurotic compulsion my mom had to be in control and somehow, in whatever possible way, inject her bragging rights into my biography, which she considered belonged to her by virtue of carrying me to term. As it sounds, an appointment baby is when an expectant mother confirms a predetermined calendar time and date for the doctor to induce labor. I can imagine my mom saying to me, as yet unborn: "You've been hogging my womb long enough; time to pack and move out. Now! I've got work to do and places to go!" Being an appointment baby is on the extreme end of the control spectrum, so to speak.

Being in control had always been an issue for my mom, going back to her childhood. By the time she graduated from Hunter, Mom was a proto-feminist, independent working woman. She made a promise to herself not to be tied down to homemaking or babysitting as the be-all of her existence, as her mother had done. My parents were married for eight years before I was conceived. I was a distraction from their routines. By the time I arrived, it was five years into the postwar era, and they had embraced the middle-class lifestyle, living in the Metropolitan Life Insurance Company–owned Stuyvesant Town housing development (less costly than the slightly upper-middle-class, tonier Peter Cooper Village across the 20th Street demarcation line). Being mid-middle-class had certain perks and drawbacks. We hired a live-in housekeeper, who spent weekday evenings awkwardly sitting quietly in our tiny six-by-four-foot kitchen doing little or nothing—daydreaming, perhaps—once her chores were completed. At bedtime she slept with me in my twelve-by-fifteen-foot bedroom until I was eleven years old.

The essay on our odd sleeping arrangement is another trauma for another time, yet here are two particularly upsetting incidents I must relate. Once I woke up in the middle of the night from a vivid dream about being suffocated under a ton of huge marshmallows to find our housekeeper sitting on top of me; it was reminiscent of Francisco Goya's famous print, *Seated Giant*. Apparently, she thought this was the only way to quiet my screams. On another evening, instead of taking her regular Saturday night off, she agreed to babysit for extra pay. I had fallen asleep and unexpectedly awoke around midnight, blithely tiptoed into the kitchen for a glass of water, and was utterly terrified—our housekeeper was nowhere to be found. Apparently, she left the apartment believing I was sound asleep for the night. I panicked until my parents returned home a few hours later. Any other parents would have fired her, I guess. Mine, however, figured I'd get over it, eventually. I did not.

My mom's control-freakiness rubbed off on me to a great extent in my teens and early twenties. To compete with her willpower, I needed to be in total protective control. Altering my appearance was one way. Moving out of the house when I was seventeen was another. This following example was the most radical of all my acting-out episodes.

My parents were not informed of my brief engagement to Pat, nor were they invited to our wedding and reception. Pat's parents weren't invited either. You can just imagine what ensued. We were married (I don't remember on what date, but it was summer 1971) at the famous St. Mark's Church in-the-Bowery. The reception afterward was thrown by Al Goldstein, my boss and publisher of *Screw* and a leading sixties cultural rabble rouser, social satirist, and pornographer (more about him later) at Ratner's Dairy Restaurant at 111 Second Avenue, next door to the Fillmore East rock palace (where I saw Jimi Hendrix on its opening night).

Pat and I were barely twenty-one years old. I really didn't consider that getting married was such a big deal. It seemed more like a prolonged bad date night where neither of us could make any lame excuses about going home early or not answering the telephone the next morning. Getting married was my way of controlling the inevitability of being rejected (which my mom managed to instill in me by taking so many "family" trips without me) and forestalling an experience I knew so well.

We followed the standard marriage protocols. Got a blood test, went down to the municipal building for the license, and hired the St. Mark's

Church in-the-Bowery's minister, local peace activist Father Garcia, to officiate at the ceremony. The only caveat was that Pat and I were required to sit through a mandatory three-hour counseling session with the minister, after which he would give us his blessing or not. Not surprisingly, he advised against our union, insisting we were too immature—and adding for good measure that rushing into marriage and, God forbid, having a child could be living hell. Nothing he said was binding. Like Ralphie in Jean Shepherd's wonderful film *A Christmas Story*, who was cautioned "you'll shoot your eye out" if he were to get a coveted Red Ryder air-powered BB gun, we ignored all prescient warnings, including those offered by our friends. So, we scheduled an appointment wedding, paid the fifty dollars, and read the rote vows that tied the (slip) knot without conviction. I invited Father Garcia to the reception at Ratner's, but he declined with an excuse similar to that of a Paul Simon lyric in "Me and Julio Down by the Schoolyard" about the "radical priest come and get me released." In fact, Father Garcia did have to bail someone out of the infamous jail known as the tombs using our fifty dollars.

I decided we would make the announcements to our respective families over the telephone a day after the wedding. Taken completely unawares, my mom cried hysterically on cue when I blurted out the news. Listening silently on the extension line, my dad showed no overt emotion, but I think he was hurt too. It was mean and cruel to notify them in this way, but in some vengeful and righteous way it was incredibly satisfying.

My mom had never met the bride and didn't even know I had a girlfriend. I had met Pat only three weeks before we decided to wed, when she worked briefly as a receptionist at *Screw*. We actually hooked up at the first (I think) gay pride parade at Sheep Meadow in Central Park. She was handing out flyers for *Screw*'s subsidiary publication, *Gay*, which I designed, and I was nonchalantly trying to bump into her. It worked.

Another problem for Mom was that Pat was a Catholic girl. Whether or not she practiced the religion was irrelevant. "It'll kill your grandmother (and your other grandparents if they were still alive)," she uttered through her tears. "How could you be so thoughtless and reckless?" "Sorry," I said, "I don't have those old-world prejudices about religious affiliation." Only a few years earlier I asked Mom how she would feel or what she might do if I married a Catholic. She only shrugged, thinking it was just idle chatter. What difference would it make? I was way too young to be thinking about such things, anyway.

Yet despite her understandable hurt and anger, after the first tidal wave of hysterics subsided, and to her credit, she seemed to suck it up and instantly invited us to the aforementioned dinner at a local restaurant for the next night. Mom's intent was to stake her position as the "mother-in-law in chief" and convey to Pat the pertinent biographical facts of her own life as quickly as possible. Because my marriage was as much about her as me. And, of course, my mom wanted Pat to call her "Mother," which was not a countercultural thing to do. And would never happen!

Neither Pat nor I looked forward to the dinner, but we were obligated. Since our main goal was to not have family in attendance at our wedding—and we succeeded—the least we could do was meet the respective families on their own turfs. My family personnel were simple enough to organize: one surviving grandmother (who I always loved very much), a mother and father, two extremely kind uncles and aunts, and four very young cousins. It turned out that, in addition to my parents, only my grandma Ray chose to meet Pat at that time (and her Catholicism did seem to be an issue).

Pat's more complex family tree was the byzantine comingling of two widowed and widowered broods, including one mother, a stepfather, a total of ten siblings—a smattering of stepkids, siblings from Pat's long-deceased biological father, and a couple of half-siblings from the union of her mother and stepfather. Pat also had a slew of aunts whose names all began with Mary-this and Mary-that, among them two habited nuns, Sisters Magdelena- and Rosalina-something, who Pat introduced to me as "my aunts." And she had a battalion of forgettable uncles and first, second, and third cousins, all blond-haired with ruddy Irish complexions. It was through Pat, incidentally, that I became the art director of the Irish Arts Center in New York. I could write an entire book on being the wandering Jew in Pat's family's suburban New Jersey backyard. Suffice to say it was no episode of *Bridget Loves Bernie*—the sixties sitcom about harmony between a mildly funny Irish and Jewish couple and their respective stereotypical families.

We went to great lengths to keep my liberal, Democratic, Manhattan, Jewish parents and Pat's devout, blue-collar, Metuchen, New Jersey, Irish Catholic relations from meeting. As it turns out, it was not difficult, save for a very short awkward telephone call. Pat's clan did not relish coming to Manhattan, but, even more consequentially, Pat's stepfather's intense dislike toward me was a handicap.

ART DIRECTOR HELLER and busty bride-to-be Pat admire steely tool.

Mr. Alvin Goldstein
and
Mr. James Buckley
are pleased to announce
the engagement of their children
Patricia Morris
and
Steven Heller
to each other

Pat Morris is going to Heller, Steve, that is. Miss Morris, who is an alumnus of the William Ward Home for Unwed Mothers, is presently serving time as an exploited woman on the editorial staff of SCREW. Mr. Heller, who is a graduate of the Famous Artists school and worked on *Rock, Inter/View* and the *New York Review of Sex and Politics* before assuming his present position as Art Director for SCREW. He is, as Miss Morris explained over the phone to her hysterical mother, "successful enough to support me in the manner to which I plan to become accustomed." In re-

sponse to queries, it was revealed that Miss Morris is not even pregnant, though Steve may be.

The plans were announced last week after a night of heavy drinking and one too many Shirley Temples for Steve. To everybody's astonishment, they were still serious the next morning, and Mr. Goldstein feted the couple with a champagne reception (domestic) in the front office. After all, the list of broken hearts, broken romances, broken homes and marriages (not to mention unhousebroken pets) which have plagued SCREW staffers is legion. Suddenly the prospect of joy in the form of a catered affair floods the office with new hope.

The wedding is planned for late summer, although Steve had hoped to have it coincide with Nixon's trip to Red China. Pat will probably have the chutzpah to wear white anyway. Until then, a busy social schedule is expected for the couple at local beer halls and massage parlours.

Wedding announcement written by Al Goldstein with his characteristic sarcasm, published in *Screw* on August 9, 1971, one month after my twenty-first birthday.

Pat's stepfather and I had not hit it off from the first handshake. He regularly had a higher-than-acceptable alcohol level, and I did not drink, suggesting to him a certain flaw in my character. During our initial, one-sided, besotted conversation, he asked about my draft status. Anticipating this, Pat forewarned me not to answer. Yet I was so cocky over my success in staying out of military service in protest of the Vietnam War that I proudly regaled him for about sixty seconds with my draft-dodging stratagems, and then...

I saw his relaxed, reclined body stiffening and his already crimson cheeks turning dark purple. He exploded like a hospital patient experiencing the dread sundown syndrome. In a split second, he grabbed my shoulders and insisted in no uncertain terms I was never "fricking" to set foot in his home again. While physically restrained by his wife, my wife, and her two brothers—the two aunts/nuns sitting shocked in a corner—my inebriated stepfather-in-law volunteered this sobering prediction: "Pat is a [handful]. I promise you that either you will split up in six months, or you'll start heavily drinking too...probably both since you're not married in the eyes of the church anyway!"

One year later, almost to the day, I wrote him the following few lines on a postcard: "Sir, you were off by six months. But I must admit your prediction was more or less accurate. We've split and I drink rye and ginger ale. Peace."

Now, back to the "appointment baby" part of this story.

One divorce and five years later, at another get-to-know-the-in-laws dinner, Mom matter-of-factly announced to Julia Goggin, my soon-to-become second wife, "Remember I told you that Steve was an 'appointment baby'?"

I'm not sure why she posed it as a question. Was it a provocation toward me? Or a meaningless breaking of the ice? I monitored all communication between my mom and Julia and was sure that Mom had not told her before.

Julia and I had already paved the way for a smooth relationship among our families. My folks and Julia's widowed mother and Vietnam vet/fireman brother, whom I liked immensely, were all invited to the wedding. And before the event, they all met and seemed to get along with one another. (Julia's closest maiden aunt from Rhode Island, a devout Catholic, declined to attend and summarily disinherited Julia because I was Jewish.) The wedding was held at a house in Hampton Bays, Long Island, that I shared with my best friend at the time, the progressive documentary video pioneer John

Reilly, and his documentarian wife, Julie Gustafson, their two small kids, and his sweet old Irish mother.

But why did my mom say, "Remember I told you?" I really think her synapses were not firing right. She either mistook Julia, wife number two, for Pat, wife number one, or for another girlfriend of mine that she'd briefly met a year earlier, who looked kind of like Julia. She was just so used to bragging about the "appointment," she assumed she'd told everyone.

Nonetheless, I was getting pretty sick of hearing this tidbit of biographical detritus. But Mom thought it was a tasty morsel. By my third, final (happy and blessedly forever) marriage to Louise, seven years after Julia and I decided to split up, it was a standard in Mom's repertoire. And since she must've told everyone, I thought that she must've already told Louise when I wasn't around.

I was wrong! A few weeks before our wedding, after a take-out chicken dinner (that my mom insisted she cooked) at my parents' home on East 36th Street, Mom said, "Before you leave, I've got to show you something incredible," and took out a box containing VHS cassettes. Recently, she had transferred ten or so Super 8 Kodak films from my dad's home-movie collection to VHS, and she couldn't wait to play a few so that Louise got to see the full-length Heller-rama epic. The cassettes contained everything from scenes of our Reformed Jewish Christmas Eve family get-togethers, to Christmas-morning (with fake miniature white tree and all) gift openings, to my lavish birthday parties, to my folks' regular biannual treks to distant exotic lands (they were in Havana immediately following the revolution, and my dad took historic footage of captured government helmets piled in huge stacks on the streets), to ocean liner departures from the West Side piers. In one of these rough-cut amateur sequences, my mom is on an upper deck of the Dutch American Lines Something-or-Other, self-consciously waving at my dad, who was dutifully filming from the deck bellow.

"Where's baby Steve?" Louise queried, assuming they would never leave their six-week-old bundle of joy behind for the three whole weeks while crossing the sea.

"He's back home with the housekeeper, of course," Mom replied. Taken aback, Louise asked, "When was this? How old was he?" Mom responded that it was almost six weeks after her legendary appointment birth, proudly adding, "It was just enough time for my figure to return to normal."

"Home?" Louise responded, "At six weeks!?"

"Why of course," Mom replied, probably unaware that contemporary clinical studies of emotional scars caused by parental abdication such as this had become a big deal in child-rearing psychology circles. "He was being looked after by the housekeeper—What-was-her-name?—and if there was a problem, she could always call Steve's [sixty-something] grandfather in the Bronx. He was just an hour away by subway." Incidentally, the housekeeper had been hired less than a month before. Also, being sixty-something in the 1950s was not as young as it is today.

Louise was still a few years away from giving birth to our son, Nick, but, as the youngest of three Italian American sisters, she was instinctively aware that leaving me with a virtual stranger was a disastrous mistake.

"Oh, my dear," Mom answered with conviction and affectation borne of watching know-it-alls on TV talk shows, "that's how it was done in those days." It was the fifties, after all. My mom had had a career and, like others of her independent/careerist ilk, followed standard practices— rules of the road, so to speak—like scheduling an appointment baby so that she could plan vacations and other recreational activities without inconvenience (or deserved guilt?).

The standard practices seemed to work. I was delivered on schedule. I was fed, bathed, and played with on schedule. And I adhered to all the cognitive and growth tables on time. I was the perfect appointment baby, except for one thing: I grew up to be nothing like whom my parents had planned or expected. Being an appointment baby—and an only child— hacked my wiring somehow.

What makes God laugh? goes the old joke: making plans. I would add: and scheduling babies. What made me laugh as a teenager was making my parents apoplectic that I was becoming a commie-hippie-rebel-without-a-cause—or, worse, with a cause.

The appointment baby, twenty-one years later. I was obsessed with having long, unkempt hair as a symbol of hippie rebellion.

CHAPTER 3

Good and Bad Hair Days

The families whom I lived with in Sweden provided my first real encounter with foreigners (albeit I was the foreigner in their country, we Americans were somehow taught that wherever an American citizen set foot was American soil). My grandparents and their families were immigrants from Eastern Europe, but they weren't foreigners to me. They had lived in New York long before I was born and in the melting pot, mulligan, potpourri, smorgasbord, poke bowl mash-up called the Bronx. In all the boroughs, but especially the Bronx, greenhorns were not outsiders, they just spoke American English with guttural, nasal, or lilting accents, no different than any other regional dialects, like those of Southerners. Instead of "bless your heart," my family said "mazel tov" or "schmuck."

In New York there was an undercurrent of racial and ethnic prejudice. Anti-Semitism was, I was led to believe, a ritual rite-of-passage or custom; it was nothing personal and didn't amount to much more than a bit of name-calling from kids who belonged to different ethnicities. When I was seven, I saw a young kid of about five walking down the street with his dad while casually giving the Hitler salute. I heard his dad say, "You know Hitler was a bad man?" The kid responded, "Oh, I thought he was a hero, like Shakespeare." Now, there was a learning moment.

I witnessed minor *West Side Story*–like scuffles between rival cliques or sophomoric individuals. But what gave me more concern than racial or ethnic tensions was that—in the midsummer of 1966, after I had returned to New York from Sweden—so many strangers, regardless of their respective heritages, went out of their way to physically and verbally attack me because my wavy black hair was unconventionally long, down to my shoulders. My hair became a lightning rod for rude comments and unwanted physical contact. I was worried for my own well-being, but nonetheless angered by their intolerance. I guess I should have been proud that my appearance seemed to unite the various urban antagonists through their common revulsion of me and my kind. But I found them downright menacing.

I got little sympathy from my mom, who accused me of igniting the discord. "You should cut your hair and this will all go away," she insisted. What's more, she harangued me almost every day with such confidence-deadening, nagging insults as "Your face is too small for all that hair" and "You look like a clown." I estimate that her words extended by at least three years my weekly private and later group psychotherapy sessions. I suffered from, among other common teenage entries in the *Diagnostic and Statistical Manual of Mental Disorders*, appearance insecurity. As it became evident that I was balding like my dad and her father before that, I am convinced my mom believed it was her redemption, although she outwardly sympathized with my self-consciousness and unhappiness over premature hair loss. (At the time my dad was going through the process of having a hair transplant, at her insistence.)

My mom had an unnatural obsession about my hair—its symbolic implications lay somewhere deep in her subconscious—and gave me the same parental "I'm telling you this for your own good" bullshit when, a year or two earlier, before the hippie movement took hold, I started wearing a greasy pomade-saturated pompadour, just like the JDs (juvenile delinquents) wore their coifs at Junior High School 104, where I briefly was enrolled in 1964. Hair symbolism is a book in itself. After returning from Sweden, I never again touched Vitalis, Brylcreem, or the hardening green hair goo we called "elephant snot" to sculpt another pompadour.

To Mom's point, wearing my hair long was socially challenging, if not dangerous. More than that, it demanded strategic thinking in order to escape the gatekeepers of fortress Stuyvesant Town, our segregated middle-class apartment housing bastion surrounded by tenement neighborhoods, without being humiliated by fellow residents. My deceit was to tie my hair into a tight ponytail and tuck it under my turtleneck shirt collar whenever I stepped out. I'd also aim my walk to the safe haven of Greenwich Village. One of my circuitous gauntlets to get there was to trot along the cobblestone parking islands that surrounded StuyTown, then down Avenue D, where Con Edison had its generators and where the JDs hung out on every corner, until I came to the even more dangerous, junkie-ridden side streets below 14th Street, where local gang members menacingly gathered in front of the delis and bodegas along Alphabet City (avenues A, B, C, and D). Then I would walk quickly through the needle-strewn park that was Tompkins Square Park (I got held up at knifepoint twice there), until I reached the crowded bustling safety of St. Marks Place. I knew I was safe when I passed Gem Spa, the putative home of the classic New York egg cream and a bohemian hangout. From there I had the right of way, past the Electric Circus and Cooper Union to Washington Square Park, which lead to MacDougal and Bleecker streets, where grungy coffeehouses beckoned. Sure, it would have been easier to cut my hair, but fuck them all! Involuntary cutting would come soon enough.

Once safely in Greenwich Village, I could usually find succor in Cafe Rienzi, Le Figaro Cafe, and a few other freak-friendly spots. If they were too crowded, I'd parade aimlessly up and down MacDougal Street with the other freaks, riffing on the tourists who came from New Jersey. Often I ended up at the digs of my oldest friend, Leigh Hart, who lived in a splendid townhouse decorated in intricate teakwood carvings, just east of Fifth Avenue on Tenth Street, north of Washington Square. The townhouse was owned by his stepfather, a printing plant owner. He was a dyed-in-the-wool anti-Semite (after he died, the building was sold to the NYU Chabad; the Orthodox Jews took their revenge) who got fairly nasty when he consumed liquor. But nonetheless he printed the first magazine I edited, an ersatz self-published literary journal, *Borrowed Time*. For most of the late summer and early fall of 1966, I basically lived rent free in the garden apartment that Leigh had commandeered—not a bad situation.

I was sixteen. Sweden had unlocked my inner hippie and showed me there was more to life than what I learned at McBurney School, the oppressive boys-only prep school. I ended up there as consequence of a psychological evaluation my parents had me endure for a weekend at an NYU testing center several years earlier. It was suggested I attend a private boy's school because I was (that magic word) "precocious." McBurney promised repro-gramming. This included wearing a wrestling team varsity letter and belong-ing to the student Kiwanis Key Club (young businessmen-in-training) like the good lad my folks intended me to be.

When summer was over, I reluctantly suspended my bohemian aspira-tions and returned to McBurney, where we wore blue blazers with embroi-dered school crests or sweaters, gray wool pants, and short cropped hair (the kind my mom loved). I was not prepared for reentry into this world, especially the part where the aptly titled "dean of discipline" named Mr. Deme, a demagogue and a stubby little despot with jowls like a gerbil, each day carefully measured the distance between every student's hair to his shirt collar with a ruler as we walked obediently past his first-floor checkpoint.

Assuming there'd be a problem, I had cut a few hairs—a trim, really—before the first day of school and greased my head down with goop. On opening day in mid-September 1966, Deme measured my fringe and ordered the first of several punitive haircuts. Each time I'd have the barber take off a few centimeters, and each time Deme hauled me out of line, until ultimately on the fourth day he grabbed my ear and roughly escorted me to a local barber who was told to cut it all off. Although I protested, Deme and the gym teacher, another Dickensian scum bucket, held me down as the barber, a sadist with an electric clipper, removed my dignity and sheared my identity. Presumably, they had the right to do this, according to the contract signed by my parents that in essence said students were not allowed to have individual dignity or identity at McBurney School.

What sealed my fate at McBurney was a bit of voodoo called a Thematic Apperception Test (TAT), a key diagnostic part of the battery at that NYU test center. For those who have never experienced a TAT, apperception (as defined by the APA Dictionary of Psychology) is

> the assimilation of a present experience based on past experiences. It is the process of drawing a relationship between new stimuli coming in from the senses and information stored in the mind through past per-ceptions.... Apperception is conscious, it is deliberate.[1]

1. *APA Dictionary*, American Psychological Association, s.v. "Thematic Apperception Test (TAT)," accessed January 3, 2922, https://dictionary.apa.org/thematic-apperception-test.

In the 1960s, as we baby boomers were hitting our pubescence, society took a turn toward the puritanical and kids were beginning to rebel against the "lamestream." For some of our "greatest generation" parents, cognitive psychology was seen as a cure. The psychologist's job was to pinpoint social evils (like girlie mags, comic books, and rock 'n' roll) then weed out and reprogram those of us children with personality defects detrimental to the postwar American dream. Armed with tests to determine mental acuity of young boomers, five psychologists worked on evaluative studies over three days to determine if I needed a behavioral tune-up. Many of these tests were visual triggers that prompted conscious or repressed subconscious responses, and one of them, the TAT, changed the course of my teenage life. According to the online Encyclopedia of Mental Disorders, the TAT (developed during the 1930s by Henry A. Murray and Christiana D. Morgan at Harvard University) "is a projective measure intended to evaluate a person's patterns of thought, attitudes, observational capacity and emotional responses to ambiguous test materials." These "ambiguous materials" involve a set of eight-by-ten cards that portray men, women, children—young and old—in random settings and menacing situations rendered in tight representational black-and-white crayon and charcoal. Unlike the inkblots in a Rorschach test, each TAT image is seeded with deliberately matter-of-fact details designed to evoke revealing personal interpretations. Encyclopedia of Mental Disorders:

> The subject is asked to tell the examiner a story about each card that includes the following elements: the event shown in the picture; what has led up to it; what the characters in the picture are feeling and thinking; and the outcome of the event.

I recall the aspects of the process vividly. It was kind of fun making up wild stories to accompany the pictures (a process I later employed when, as art director at the *New York Times Book Review*, I asked famous authors to "illustrate" drawings in words rather than the more conventional other way around). Little did I know that during the TAT I was under a microscope.

Recently, I was reminded of one card—the very one (see illustration) that I believe changed the person I would become. If this sounds like melodrama, think about any art, music, or writing that has changed your life. I've been influenced by many images, sounds, and words, but, unbeknownst to me, my future hinged on my response to that TAT. My parents had "paid good money for the test, and we're not going to ignore the findings," they told me. To this day I recall the narrative conjured by this seminal TAT image. It was a story so absurd and maladroit yet perceived by the testers as so perverse. Being branded in the final evaluation as "precocious" ("indicative of early development") was ridiculous because I had no idea what I was talking about. I merely acquired and repeated vernacular from the street.

I was barely twelve (in fact, I was eleven and a half) and had little or no knowledge of life's taboos, mysteries, or pleasures, save for a few grade school hygiene classes. (I had not yet read Henry Miller's *Tropic of Cancer*, and J. D. Salinger's *The Catcher in the Rye* was on the following year's reading list.) But somehow a TAT drawing triggered an untapped flow of libido. The fateful picture was of a woman lying half naked in bed with a clothed man standing beside her. He had turned away with his hand covering his eyes. Was he ashamed? Guilty? Or self-satisfied? This image turned my raging hormones on the same way the sensuous Maidenform bra ads in the *New York Times Magazine*

My "precocious" response to this TAT image convinced my parents to send me to an all-boy prep school, McBurney.

did for most boys my age (and many older ones too). The curious narrative I concocted was a convoluted, innocently deviant fantasy that ended in my own uncontrollable nervous laughter. I won't reveal the story because it is still embarrassing, but at the time I thought I was clever in turning what appeared to be a tragic scenario into a sex comedy that today would have been apt as a scene in an HBO miniseries. The test giver couldn't stop me from laughing; pages of notes filled his yellow pad.

I'm still unclear why an eleven-and-a-half-year-old would be exposed to such prurient imagery, or why this and the other pictures in the TAT were also so damn lugubrious. The test remains clear in my mind, even now. But how was I to know that my response to bizarre, kinky stuff that I knew nothing about was inappropriate—triggered, no doubt, by being mentally poked and prodded by grad psych students during that two-hour portion of a three-day exam in a windowless NYU examination room?

Weeks afterward, a manila envelope containing the evaluations arrived in the mail. My parents retreated to their bedroom and closed the door so they could review the contents in private. After an hour of silent reading and soft whispers, they were mum about the findings. But I knew that the results of the TAT were why I was banished to an all-boy's prep school instead of a co-ed high school (where I would have been much happier and less riddled by angst) and why they insisted I could not have girls come to visit when no parent was home. Many years later, as I was rifling through my father's dresser looking for loose change, I accidentally stumbled on the long-forgotten evaluation. Here's the gist:

The subject is an above average intelligent twelve-year-old [couldn't they get my age straight?]. However, he appears to be precocious for a child of his age. He either understands what he's saying or mimics what he has heard from others....It is our recommendation that he attend a strict high school with defined parameters...and play lots of exertion sports.

Testing has a place in understanding childhood development, yet I continue to question its efficacy. As reported in *Psychological Science in the Public Interest* (2000):

Like other projective techniques, the TAT has been criticized on the basis of poor psychometric properties....Criticisms include that the TAT is unscientific because it cannot be proved to be valid or reliable....As stories about the cards are a reflection of both the conscious and unconscious motives of the storyteller, it is difficult to disprove the conclusions of the examiner and to find appropriate behavioral measures that would represent the personality traits under examination.

So much for modern psychology and apperception evaluations. Even given the best intentions, what I endured was replete with idiotic suggestions and fool's promises. But I admit that I still get a kick out of the illustration that triggered my entire odyssey.

When I returned to the McBurney School student population on the day I was shorn, I was almost bald and had earned a few bonus detention demerits in the bargain. Stoically, I held back the tears until I returned home, where I erupted into breakdown-strength hysteria. I refused to leave the house indefinitely thereafter. To my parents' credit, they were angered by the breach of personal freedom, but their cure was to buy me a hat. They sent me back to school. I quit the wrestling team and Kiwanis Key Club, and at the end of the school day returned directly home. For three months I never left the confines of my apartment except to go to school.

There was a plus side to staying at home. I started to obsessively draw pictures of my feelings with pen, India ink, and Dr. Ph. Martin's dyes. My Uncle Walter, appalled by the haircutting incident, recommended that I see a shrink who handled "gifted kids with crippling neurosis." He insisted that my parents send me to see her or else they would certainly watch my descent into a very dark place. Drawing and reading books about drawing and looking at drawings and cartoons—especially Jules Feiffer's *Village Voice* cartoons and Harvey Kurtzman's *Little Annie Fannie* comics in *Playboy*—and poring through *Mad* magazine were my saving (albeit contraband) graces.

As a diversion, I had long drawn pictures of war and Western scenes and narrated them as I drew them, like cinematic storyboards. But in my post-haircut life I was going deeper into my psyche to express the repressed anger and deep depression that my shrink said I had nurtured toward the world in general and my parents, teachers, and others in authority in particular, the degrees of which would be determined later. I did feel comfortable with one faculty member at McBurney, the drama teacher, named Mr. Bates (we called him Master Bates). A former B-picture actor whose big role was an extraterrestrial scientist in a science-fiction horror movie, he taught us about the world's religions but was the most liberal of all the McBurney pedagogic miscreants. He wore an ND (nuclear disarmament) button, which technically was not allowed. I learned that buttons were a good way to protest things. I bought one that read "Enemy of the State," which disturbed my parents, particularly my father, who worked in the Office of Inspector General for the US Air Force. He was under routine FBI scrutiny, I later learned, because of my underground doings, when he applied for a new job in the federal government.

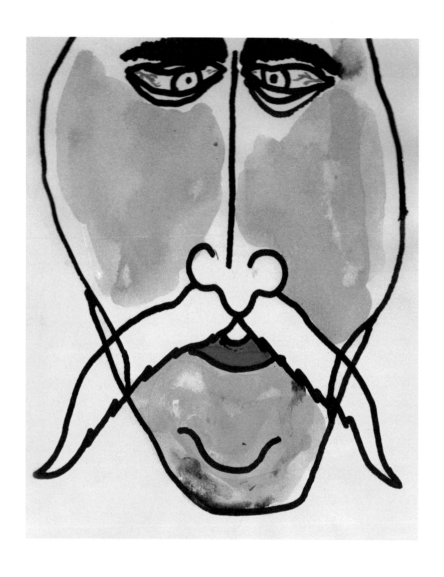

My interpretation of Frodo, J. R. R. Tolkien's most renowned character, which
I drew on T-shirts that I sold to students at McBurney School, circa 1965.

Influenced by Aubrey Beardsley and other European Symbolists
I had found in books and underground newspapers, I spent much of my free time
drawing mostly demonic castrated men as a response the trauma of having my hair
forcibly shorn by the dean of discipline at McBurney School, circa 1966.

My drawings soon became the main topic of my twice-weekly therapy sessions. You'll understand why after I describe the themes: little naked men without genitals, adorned with long Jesus-inspired hair and thick mustaches, often hanging on crucifixes or crouched over toilet bowls, puking their guts out. I drew other characters later, and all involved the removal of limbs or women with extremely sumptuous breasts. Sometimes I'd be more prosaic, drawing trees struggling to hold onto their leaves and bending in opposite directions against strong winds. Other drawings included prisoners behind walls, bars, and other impediments. Pretty obvious symbolism, no?

Since I liked Aubrey Beardsley's work—he was the nineteenth-century symbolist artist who had become popular during the hippie era—I drew backgrounds that were made up of contoured and circuitous black, entangled lines. Everything was representational but nothing was realistic—and frankly, I wasn't certain what they all meant until the shrink and I reviewed and deconstructed them. As an artist I wasn't that good when compared to illustrators of professional magazines, but the shrink was so enamored by my work that I felt more confident. I gave her a few as gifts.

As for technique, mostly I used crow quill pen points dipped into Winsor & Newton India ink and prismatic liquid colors that I blended to look like sunsets and mystical auras. Sometimes I made rain that turned the pictures gray. The drawings not only kept me occupied, but they also gave me back what McBurney had stolen; they defined who I was and what I was about to become.

To my unhappy surprise, my mom said that she loved, or at least was morbidly fascinated by, the drawings. She always wanted to co-opt my work and show it off to her friends. She begged me to leave my portfolio around so when people visited she could crow contentedly (like she did with her travel slides and 8 mm movies). My work was reduced to a trophy of her motherhood. I resented her intrusion into my private world. Years later, with my reluctant permission, she cut some of them up and laminated them as a collage onto a coffee tabletop. As soon as both my parents passed away, I found and disposed of that table along with dozens of albums of their travel snapshots. I gave some of my surviving drawings to my son, Nick, who showed an honest interest in them.

While I was finding solace in art, my hair was growing back centimeter by centimeter. My interest in leaving the house was slowly returning, but most important my father was, in his quiet way, secretly attempting to get me into a less toxic school environment. I'll always love him for this act of kindness. He succeeded in convincing the Walden School, a New York Upper West Side progressive private school, to accept me in the middle of my junior year against their stated policy. I remember the afternoon he called me at home to tell me the news. I was never as ecstatic as in that single moment.

Walden had no corrosive rules. We could wear what we wanted. We called the teachers by their first names. It was co-ed. Girls! I could meet and spend time with girls!

Walden welcomed individuality. The school's headmaster, Nate Levine, said the only uniform we wore was "a uniform of alienation." (I later realized it was one of the cleverest backhanded put-downs I'd ever heard, but it sounded refreshing at the time.) Acceptance meant I would start right after Christmas break, so my remaining weeks at McBurney reminded me of the time my parents let me draw all over the walls of my room because they were having the apartment painted. The Walden art teacher told me he liked my drawings and wanted me to do linocuts for the school yearbook in my faux Beardsley style. I had gotten on the stairway to heaven.

On my last day at McBurney, I bid a very fond good-bye to Master Bates (never saw him again), simply ignored Mr. Deme-God, and, as my last act of retribution, spat right in the gym teacher's face, smiled, and walked away. He was so shocked he just stood there speechless and motionless. I have no idea what he did or said when he came to his senses, but, man, was that so satisfying.

I told my father. He looked at me sternly and asked with a hint of pride, "You did that? Really?" Then he hid a faint smile and went back to reading his *Consumer Reports* magazine. He and I still had violent disagreements over the Vietnam War until well into the sixties, when I was of draft age, but from then on I realized my dad was always on my side, one way or another.

CHAPTER FOUR

The Impossible Dream

T he McBurney reprieve changed my deeply dour teenage life and ended my descent into Dante's nine rings of high school hell. It was a dream come true. If I still had any doubts about the miracle of redemption, I became an unequivocal believer in a divine power when a second impossible dream came true. I was on a good karma roll.

Many years earlier I had a vicarious crush on a child actress-model who appeared in scores of ubiquitous commercials for the advertisers and sponsors of dozens of Saturday morning network TV kids' shows. These fantasies were in no way overtly erotic—I simply daydreamed that we were going steady—and like the lyric of so many pop songs, I imagined that "she wore my ring." I was realistic enough to know she was an unattainable obsession. Dreaming, wishing, or praying was not going to make our relationship real. She was so pretty; she was the quintessential embodiment of blemish-free American perfection, the talisman on commercials for toys, dolls, games, cereal, and more. She was a familiar, welcome presence on all the television shows from when she was six, seven, or eight years old until she was, say, around eleven or twelve years old. Then she just disappeared. I reasoned she was the victim of "old age." I forgot about her.

Until one night. As it happened, I was home alone while my parents were off on one of their long vacations. I was watching Johnny Carson's *Tonight Show* when, near the signoff at around one a.m.—the time most networks aired their mandatory pro bono public service commercials—I saw an oldie that had played a few years earlier. I remembered it vividly. It featured a young boy and girl sitting on a building stoop reciting their lines in a call and response singsong manner: "Mayor Wagner does it," said the boy, "Mickey Mantle does it," said the girl. "Willie Mays does it," and so forth. After a couple more names, together they looked directly at the camera, smiled, and in unison uttered the catchline: "They all pitch in for a cleaner New York."

It was the girl!

The very same actress I had such a crush on from those Saturday morning commercials. Since this PSA was produced a few years before, I presumed that she was older and gorgeous too in the well-scrubbed, bright-eyed way that typified an American ideal. She was my ideal. I wondered if she were still an actress. Remembering my vintage memories, I drifted off into a deep sleep.

I can tell you she was, indeed, older and gorgeous! The most beautiful girl ever. How did I know? After all, there was no Google image search engine in 1966. It was like being in the most remarkable dream anyone could ever hope to have.

The reality, however, goes like this. The very next evening, that girl on TV walked into my parents' apartment. I wasn't hallucinating or delusional (I didn't do any drugs, then or ever). Yes, she was older. Yes, she was a striking redhead, wearing red lipstick with a TV model's smile. If I hadn't believed in a merciful God before, this marvel certainly cinched the deal.

As random as this visitation might seem, it was not as divine as walking on water, making fishes into loaves, or curing the blind. I was friends with quite a few kids who were working in show business. (I even tried auditioning, but gave up after failing to get any parts, even walk-ons.) My friends went to the Professional Children's School or the Lincoln Square schools established for professional child actors, musicians, singers, and dancers. One of the inevitabilities of growing up in New York's private-schooled, middle-class social circle was being classmates or teammates or party friends or steadies with the children of famous people or befriending kids who were themselves moderately famous in roles on TV soaps or Broadway theater. At McBurney my friends included Chris Roberts, son of Pernell Roberts of *Bonanza*; Jason Robards III, son of actor Jason Robards Jr.; Keith Kaufman, son of Murray Kaufman (Murray the K), WINS disc jockey and the so-called fifth Beatle; and Richard Thomas, who the year after leaving McBurney School became John Boy, star of the hit show *The Waltons* on CBS. I hung out for a while with Mia Farrow's younger sister Tisa and quite a few other kids who then or later became actors and show business personalities.

One such friend, Jan Rhodes—a fifteen-year-old aspiring singer-actress and the daughter of a veteran Broadway performer—would occasionally stop by my apartment. Jan's best friend was Virginia (Chicky) Mason, that girl on the Saturday commercials. Her divorced stage mom had left her job as a commercial artist (I had no idea what that was) to manage her daughter's brief though successful and, I assumed, lucrative career. Jan and I went out from time to time but were not exclusive. We'd make out, mostly. It was a coincidence that on that night, after I'd watched the old PSA, she brought Chicky to my house on the chance we'd make a nice couple. We did.

Coincidence or fate? I don't believe that it was a coincidence, but I'm skeptical about fate. It was generous of Jan, I'll say that.

Chicky was the first girl whom I ever loved who loved me back. We spent all our free time together. Life seems to go more slowly when you're that age; in fact, we were together only six or seven months before an argument lead to a sad breakup. I still think fondly of those times with her.

Five years later, following my split with my first wife, Pat, feeling wistful I hired a private detective to locate Chicky. I heard that she had left New York, possibly for Los Angeles. For my birthday that year Al Goldstein, my boss at *Screw*, offered to let me use his personal private eye. It turns out he was incompetent, and after four months he hadn't found a single trace. Chicky was not listed with the American Federation of Television and Radio Artists, the television actor's union. She had disappeared from my life forever.

After the breakup with Chicky, I hooked up with a new girlfriend, a sophomore at Walden. I was a senior. As I had been awkward with girls prior to this year—in part because being in a boy's school didn't provide much opportunity to learn the ropes—this new relationship was another minor miracle.

I think one reason for the sophomore's attraction to me had to do with my status around school as "the moody artist." Despite the fact that there were better artists in my grade, the art teacher, Neil Shevlin, was attracted to my work because his paintings, like my drawings, were abrasively surreal and psychologically disturbing. He showed his own paintings to only a few of the students whom he was confident would appreciate them. He was a great teacher, but his work so clearly revealed a deeply troubled soul that I wasn't surprised to learn that he committed suicide a few years after I graduated. His death was such a waste. I wonder how many artists have taken their own lives over their art, when they could have used art as a lifesaver?

Neil's encouragement in my senior year at Walden gave me the guts to show my portfolio to four or five underground newspaper art editors, and they began publishing a few of my cartoons. As it happened, I had earlier tried selling my work (I would have given it away) to the *New Yorker* and *Evergreen Review*, and lack of success there begat a brief period of paralytic discouragement. By the last few months of my senior year at Walden, I felt confident enough with the music concert and other posters I did for classmates and the literary magazine and yearbook covers I made for Walden to knock on the doors of the *Rat*, *New York Free Press* (the *Freep*), *Other Scenes*, *WIN* (published by the Workshop in Nonviolence), and other political tabloids. The biggest and most renowned of the alternatives, the *East Village Other* (*EVO*)—which featured comics stars R. Crumb, Spain Rodriguez, Gilbert Shelton, Kim Deitch, and more—had already turned me down, but I was pub-

Attending Walden School was the best thing that happened to me, 1966.

lished in the *Rat*, the next biggest. *Rat's* art director was Bob Eisner, who followed me to *Screw* and the *New York Times* and ended up at *Newsday*, Long Island's prominent daily.

The week after I graduated from high school, I was offered a job at the *Free Press* doing paste-ups (I had no idea what they were) by its art director (I had no idea what that title signified). He was a stout, mellow gent with an indefinable accent named J. C. Suares, and he sat at his desk drinking from a quart bottle of malt liquor.

I had asked him to review my portfolio, which he told me to leave on a chair and go away. The next day, he called my StuyTown number. Our housekeeper (the same woman who left me alone in the middle of the night and sat on me while I was sleeping), who was known not only to transcribe messages wrong but also to hold onto them for days, mistakenly told me that someone from the *New York Times* (not the *New York Free Press*) had called. Fortunately, I called the *Freep* back and talked to J. C., who told me about the job doing mechanicals.

He didn't care that I had no idea what a mechanical was; he'd teach me. In fact, he hired me so he could dump the paste-up woman who actually knew what she was doing. I don't know why he fired her. My lesson took about half an hour. I truly sucked at doing paste-up, applying two coats of rubber cement and wax, the common practice. J. C. was drawing the cartoons and caricatures for the *Freep* and had no intention of running my artwork. It's not that it was any better than his—it definitely wasn't—but it was different.

Fortuitously for me, the *Freep*'s tough-as-nails editor, Sam Edwards, seemed to appreciate my drawings. In his early thirties and an uncanny Ernest Hemingway doppelganger, Sam was both a bartender in Greenwich Village and former editor of *Arts* magazine. He offered me a weekly spot he called "A Heller" in addition to an occasional cover. He called me "the kid." I liked that.

J. C. left the *Free Press* three weeks after hiring me. He went to launch a satire magazine called *Inkling*, which was purportedly funded but never came out. Nonetheless, it started him off on an influential career in art directing. I became the *Freep*'s de facto art director. I would never have guessed that a career would follow. But my work at the *Freep* was an adventure that altered every step I took thereafter.

While most undergrounds were located downtown in the East Village, the *Free Press* was uptown on 72nd Street (across from Sherman Square and the nearby Verdi Square, known jointly in the 1960s and 1970s by local drug users and dealers as "Needle Park"). The *Freep* was originally called the

THE NEW YORK FREE PRESS

15¢
At All
Newstands

At Walden I was encouraged to do more drawings, which I showed to the *New York Free Press*, where I was hired to do layouts and illustrations, circa 1967.

(Above and Opposite) I was fixated on notions of persecution and mortality. I was not clinically depressed, but my cartoons had a definite—if self-indulgent—dark, melancholic side, 1967.

Westside News and was a community paper, not an upstart, leftie, hippie, sex, drugs, and rock 'n' roll tabloid. It was more like the *Village Voice* for the Upper West Side. Sam's aim was to be a muckraker of real city scandals, and he published some seasoned writers with solid reputations, including the Bertolt Brecht scholar Eric Bentley, art critic Gregory Battcock, *Times* film critic Roger Greenspun, JFK-assassination theorist Mark Lane, and others in the Old Left and New Left of the day. The paper attracted some interesting people, including its advertising manager, the elegant Sue Graham Ungaro, who was the on-and-off girlfriend and later wife of the jazz genius Charles Mingus. In fact, since Sue and I shared an office, she used to ask me to answer the phone when she thought Charles was calling and tell him she wasn't there. Charles would always ask my name, and this prompted my taking on the first of many pseudonyms (John Bingham was this one) to act as interference between the volatile couple. Charles routinely came up to the office; remarkably, Sue was always somewhere else. One day, he got so infuriated by her absence he smashed his sizable bassist's hand into the wall next to my smallish (as my mom reminded me) head. I came to appreciate his passion and his music. His anger, however, was intimidating.

The *Free Press* was my college. As mentioned, I was enrolled at NYU and went to the occasional class there until I left and enrolled at SVA, but I much preferred being on 72nd Street plying my new craft to going to school. At college I was headed, as the beatnik character Maynard G. Krebs in *The Many Loves of Dobie Gillis* would say, to "nowheresville." At the *Freep*, I had somewhere to go and something to believe in, although I was politically immature.

During 1968 and '69 I found different ways to make personal political commentary. (Top) I targeted how advertising manipulated people. (Middle) I•KONPAPER was an underground zine that allowed me to lambaste the idea of religious imprisonment. (Bottom) My take on a well-known military cadence, depicting police brutality toward peace demonstrators.

ᴄ*My Mentor*

With the *Freep*, in 1968 I acquired a full-time (occasionally) paid job and by chance a reluctant mentor. Brad Holland answered my ad for illustrators for a magazine I decided to edit, publish, and launch on my own. He was not seeking a job as mentor—he was seven years older than I—but once our paths crossed, fate stepped in. Without a design or art education, I was in desperate need of his wisdom and experience. Sometimes, I still need it. I could never draw or paint as well as he does. He is a natural. So, the most important takeaway I got from him focused on the ethics of making art.

I learned about aesthetics from my Walden School art teacher, Neil Shevlin, but ethics was a new subject. Brad taught me that an illustrator, a cartoonist, and even an art director could make a decisive contribution not only to a publication, but also to the culture at large (however small that culture might be). Brad offered inspiration to me when I anxiously wanted to be an artist but was indoctrinated into believing that commercial art was a lesser form. Brad convinced me otherwise.

I met Brad by accident. I started my magazine with my bar mitzvah money set aside for college tuition, which I wasn't going to need after I left

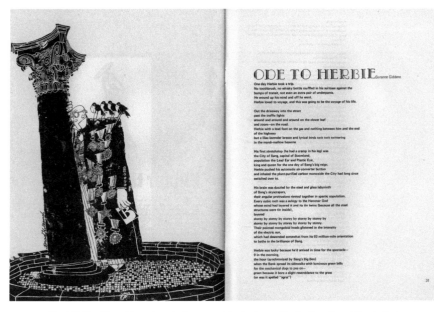

Brad Holland taught me how to be a graphic designer. He designed and illustrated this spread from my self-published magazine *Borrowed Time*, 1968.

school. Its title was *Borrowed Time*, which came from my adolescent musings on mortality and impermanence gleaned from my high school existentialist reading list—Albert Camus and Jean-Paul Sartre—and was wordplay on *Time* magazine. I had a classmate, Walden's resident Mod, who, when I floated the idea of a magazine, immediately drew a Beardsley-inspired cover of a clock (Beardsley and art nouveau had become groovy then), which to my eye was just perfect. I assembled a few poems and short stories, and I paid my best friend Leigh Hart's alcoholic, anti-Semitic stepfather to print it. At the *Freep* I had a place to set type for free on an IBM MT/ST magnetic-tape computer. I was already the seasoned art director of the *Free Press* for all of three months. How difficult could self-publishing a magazine be? Well, it wasn't as easy as I had imagined. My classified advertisement in the *Village Voice* pulled a literary/poetry/art ensemble whose gifts were inconsistent at best. Brad brought a strong point of view and heaps of talent.

Brad had arrived in New York City from Kansas City a year before, by way of Tulsa, Oklahoma, and Fremont, Ohio. He had worked as a design supervisor in what he called "the rabbit department" of Hallmark Cards in Kansas City, and he started getting hired for illustration work almost

Brad Holland and I fought over this 1968 cover illustration by Timothy Jackson. I loved the symbolism; he thought it was simpleminded. It was, however, *my* magazine.

immediately after getting off the Greyhound bus. He did not have to submit work to my semiliterate magazine and he almost didn't when he saw the content I was planning, especially the cover.

At our first meeting in Leigh's basement apartment on East Tenth Street, Brad arrived with the largest portfolio case I had ever seen. He was tall and skinny, and he sported a short beard. Like a drawing of a stereotyped rube on the cover of the *Saturday Evening Post*, just off the bus from the Midwest, he looked out of place in hippie Greenwich Village, except for his beard. Originally from Arkansas, he had worked as a supervisor at Hallmark but had come to New York to make a different kind of mark. During the hour we were together he uttered only a few words; his searing eyes never once looked directly at me but were fixed intently on his work as I slowly turned over the large, inked drawing boards.

"Good stuff," I told him holding my awe in check at the sight of his meticulously rendered line drawings featuring surreal fantasies and allegorical scenes. "I like 'em. But can you illustrate literature? Can you stick close to the text?"

Literature, indeed! I had no idea what I was talking about. Nonetheless, Brad agreed to contribute—and for no fee—so long as he retained complete control over what he did. He was like the architect Howard Roark in the book on individualism that everyone—left, right, center—was reading, *The Fountainhead* by Ayn Rand. Of course, I agreed to his demand.

I was surprised that he returned a week later for the first editorial meeting, where I would explain the magazine to the anointed contributors. Brad patiently listened to my pedantic monologue about the blah blah blah philosophy of *Borrowed Time*. He even stuck around until everyone had left, at which point he said, "I'll help you design this thing."

"But I already have an art director," I replied, referring to my artiste buddy, Timothy Jackson, who pretended to know how to produce layouts.

"He doesn't know shit about designing a magazine," Brad replied. "And frankly, you don't know much about putting a magazine together either, so I'd like to be involved at least where my drawings are concerned."

His words pierced my ego like rusty X-Acto blades. After that exchange, I wasn't sure I wanted him around, but he was persistent. He was also correct about my so-called art director, who resigned the day after we started pasting up the first pages. Brad took over the job by default, and the first thing he did was to introduce me, slowly and patiently, to real typography.

That's when Brad became my teacher—not in the ways of illustration, but in publication design in general and visual thinking specifically. He had worked for major professional art directors, Art Paul at *Playboy* and Herb Lubalin at *Avant Garde*. They were, in addition to fluent with art, brilliant typographers. I wanted to be that too. Sitting on Brad's grungy Lower East Side tenement floor day after day for three or more weeks, pasting up pages for *Borrowed Time*, cutting and gluing various clip-art letters together, making the best use of transfer and press type, I learned aspects of type use I hadn't appreciated before. Notably, I learned to achieve expression through letters and their accents, voices, and pitches—that is, the expression that different faces bring to text and headlines. I can't say that I became good at typography, but I became aware of the nuances that make it personal to each designer.

Brad did all the type composition himself. Using the great ad and magazine designer Lubalin as his model and *Avant Garde* magazine as his prime example (Brad had published his first major editorial illustration there in 1968); he showed me the emotional nuances achieved by smashing, overlapping, and otherwise allowing type to speak. While I resented that he was so much better than me at setting type—in fact, everything about graphic design—I knew that what he was imparting was the equivalent of months, possibly years, of art school training. I was torn between feeling gratitude and other, baser emotions.

I admired Brad's passion and listened spellbound as he told me about his duels with editors and art directors over his principle to never render anyone else's ideas—editor, author, or art director. Doing so was a common practice at that time. Rather, his job was to find a better, more personal solution to an illustration problem. He never illustrated anything verbatim but always reinterpreted a text in metaphorical or allegorical visual terms. Moreover, he stuck to his guns, sometimes at the expense of losing a job, which happened from time to time. His actions seemed foolhardy, profes-sional suicide. Yet when they paid off—when something without equal was published in a national magazine or on a book jacket or a poster—the result was awesome. I understood that Brad was not only fighting the conventional wisdom that an illustrator was merely the extension of an art director's or, worse, an editor's hands, he was also trying to radically alter, if not expunge,

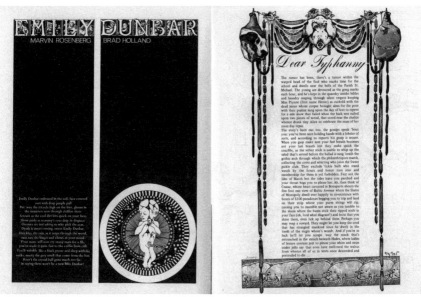

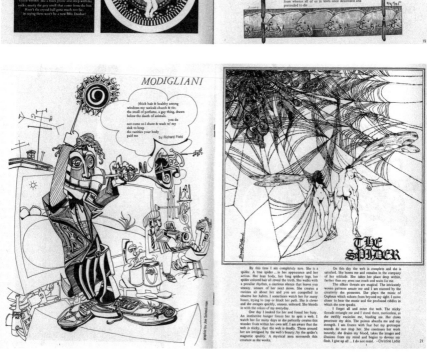

All *Borrowed Time* spreads were designed and pasted up by Brad Holland. I watched
and learned. The drawings at top left and bottom right came from his portfolio.
Top right was my introduction to nineteenth-century clip art. And the drawing at bottom
left was done by Joe Schenkman, a cartoonist I had met at the *Free Press*, 1967.

The front side of the mailing card that Brad Holland and I designed for the Asylum Press (Brad drew the "Feed Mr. Zip" stamp), 1969–70.

the conventions of slavishly sentimental illustration and create a more intimate personal art. He once confided that he would either win or quit—there was no middle ground. His plan worked! Within the year that I met him, Brad had sinecure in *Playboy* illustrating the monthly Ribald Classics section, in *Evergreen Review*, and even in the staid *Redbook* women's magazine. He eventually became a star artist for the *New York Times* Op-Ed page. Drawing inspiration from the legacies of such acerbic graphic artists as the Weimar-era graphic commentators Käthe Kollwitz, George Grosz, and Heinrich Kley, and especially from *The Disasters of War* prints by his revered Francisco Goya, Brad's stark black-and-white "idea" drawings raised the conceptual bar of an antiquated field that in America was rooted in old-school Rockwellian representation and *Saturday Evening Post* sentimentality. But just as he refused to be dictated to by editors and art directors, he was never content with having a single signature style. He told me,

My model was always writers, guys who could write essays, poetry, plays, whatever they choose, and try different approaches. There's no reason an artist can't take a similar approach. Use charcoal one day and bright colors the next. Do a series of white-on-white paintings and then do a handful of messy drawings as if you were five years old. I mean, you can't get everything into a single picture. Every picture is

very month can be Walpurgisnacht with a subscription to The Asylum Press. Witness:

The visual perversions of Steven Heller as he gropes his way through puberty &/or art school,

The nasty little pictures of Yossarian as he thirsts for world domination & crosses interstate lines to make enemies.

The photos of Joseph ("Five-Eyes") Stevens as he stakes out his claim to Second Avenue,

The unhealthy fantasies of D.A. Latimer & Ray Schultz, discoverers of the Peter principle,

The ranting & raving of Brad Holland as he parades his medieval demons in public & goes looking for Norweigan Wood.

For a fee of five dollars a year you can subscribe to this proposterous service & receive our junkmail once a month to decorate your publication with.

Each packet will contain:

- Drawings & cartoons of varied quality
- Special features such as posters, underground crossword puzzles & God's own telephone number
- All-purpose junkdrawings done by members of the Asylum Press while on a bummer in Boston
- Pornograph records
- Special advertisements for such basement products as
  SPLAT the X-tra strength floor remover
  New RAID sandwich spread
  FOOLSGOLD the killer weed "You can take FOOLSGOLD out of the country but you can't get back in with it
  AXIOM the miracle detergent with new improved TOXIN
  MOMMA WOLFGANG'S birthday spaghetti
  THE INFAMOUS ARTISTS SCHOOL complete with free "Draw Me" talent test, &
  The new G-rated THE RAT WHO ATE 42ND STREET
- STOP THE WAR ON PUBERTY decals
- Insertable promotion pieces for the usual causes
- YOUR SLUM-LOVE IT OR SHOVE IT decals
- Roadmaps showing how to get to where its at
- Hip & groovy new underground dress patterns complete with unauthorized PETER MAX stencils
- Mug shots of the Asylum Press being busted for mail fraud.

All artwork enclosed in this initial packet is free for reproduction & may be ripped off so long as the appropriate credits are included to support our egos. Full-size camera-ready copies may be ordered for 50 cents a drawing.

All money will be sacrificed to the Post Office to feed Mister Zip.

---

will risk $5 on this insane service & contribute to Mister Zip's welfare . . .

Name of person interested _____

Publication _____

Address _____

Zip Code _____

I can't make heads or tails out of this miniature artwork & would like to receive useable copies. I am willing to spend 50 cents for each drawing . . .

Names of drawings _____

_____

_____

_____

We are a legitimate business deduction.

The back side of the card contained a list of Asylum Press's goals, promises, and principles, 1969–70. All the spot art came from clip-art books. The type was set on an IBM Selectric.

just a piece of a whole. It's kind of like the old cliché of the blind guys feeling the elephant. Every day you feel a new part of who you are.

And so, he evolved his methods and manners to suit his needs, often surprising—sometimes shocking—those who commissioned him thinking they would get one thing and then wound up with another.

I wished I had Brad's talent and his courage. Frankly, the frustration of being limited by own meager capabilities was a painful struggle. I couldn't draw realistically if my life depended on it. Brad could. I couldn't come up with the visual metaphors that seemed to flow from Brad with ease. Yet at the time I continued to draw my little cartoons, and I got them published with some success in various underground newspapers. Getting published was satisfying, but more important to me was earning Brad's approval for what I was doing. I wanted his validation that my art was good. But he never said this in as many words to my face—at least I never heard him say this—so, at age eighteen I decided not to draw anymore.

Sounds childish, but I presumed that since I couldn't compete with Brad, who was not yet nearly at the top of his game, and since I liked art directing, I'd just stop doing one and focus on the other. It was a sound career move. But I also figured that if I stopped drawing, I'd be spiting him, not me. Six months after I had published my last cartoon (for a few years), I met Brad in the street.

"How come I don't see your drawings anymore?" he inquired.

"I decided to stop doing them," I said, with a discernably angry edge to my voice.

"Too bad, some of them were really good," he conceded.

Victory!

Brad and I joined forces with the underground cartoonist Yossarian and hatched a plan to conquer the alternative art and cartoon world with our work. Yossarian, the nom de crayon derived from a character in Joseph Heller's *Catch-22* of Alan Shenker, was a former post office worker who created absurdist comics about weird fetishistic themes, including the recreational use of hot lead enemas and a satiric strip called *Funny Nazis*. He also published *The Razor's Edge*, a fetish fanzine for women who shaved their heads bald and the men who loved them. I tried hard to balance my imbalanced talent on his and Brad's shoulders but found it too difficult to compete, so I committed to being Asylum Press's art director.

The Asylum Press, aptly named because we rented (or rather inhabited without paying rent) a spacious Union Square office from a somewhat crazy man. He was a professional rag man, and who wouldn't be crazy selling rags for a living? He kept a telephone at the office, and our only responsibility was to take messages and orders for him—fifty pounds one day, a hundred pounds the next.

We added Snail Studio to the Asylum Press name because it spoke to a sense of lethargy that we falsely espoused. We were actually über-motivated—but I liked the idea of a snail.

Our plan was to offer subscriptions, akin to newspaper syndication services, to underground papers and then regularly supply them with our work. It was to be used however they wanted. Brad's drawings were already lifted by underground papers around the world. Yossarian enjoyed a modest fan base too. I just wanted some recognition for anything.

The first packet was our loss leader. We paid for the production and printing. Each of us pasted up our own pages, and Brad did the "corporate identity." We made a few hundred of the first (and only) offering and sent it to every underground paper we could. Then we waited for the landslide of return subscription cards to arrive in the mail. And we waited… and waited.

Brad's work, predictably, was used, more so than before. Indeed, who wouldn't steal the opportunity? It was like getting free food at a record label publicity party. Yossarian's didn't move too much. Mine were predictably ignored.

Still, I wouldn't have missed the experience for the world. I learned not to be an illustrator or a cartoonist, while I never lost my love of illustration and cartoon. For a brief moment we were going to conquer the world with our wit, talent, and tenacity, which is all anyone really wants—just that one glorious moment. (Or maybe the US Postal Service, known for delaying certain contraband mail, was holding back the cards and jerking with our heads!?)

The Asylum experience convinced me to put my drawing pens and brushes in cold storage. As an art director I could flex my muscles. I was under Brad's watchful eye, but I was not in direct competition with him. I encouraged him to teach me about the history of satiric art and visual commentary—the same history that nourished him for many years. Brad also became a regular contributor to underground papers I designed—the

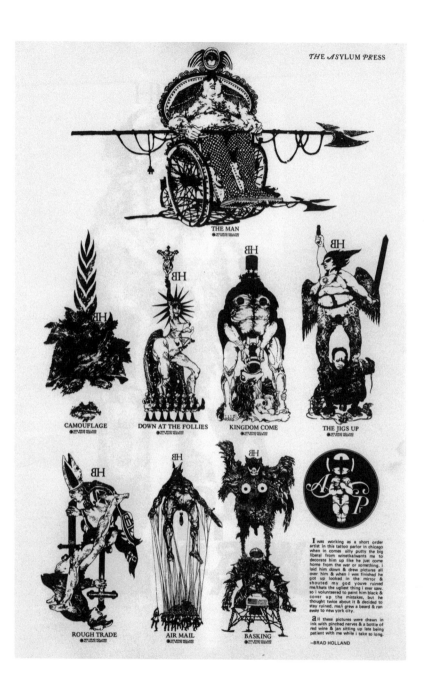

In each Asylum Press envelope was included a two-sided sample of
our respective work, 1969–70. Brad used complex pen-and-ink drawings
that he had made for the *New York Review of Sex*.

I filled my page with Jules Feiffer-inspired panel-less cartoons that
I had published in underground papers, 1969-70. We encouraged other
underground papers to print the work for free.

Drawings by Yossarian (aka Alan Shenker), who made brush-drawn comic strips
for many undergrounds, 1969–70. We shared an office for a year.

Brad Holland and I devised a branding slogan (although we did not call it branding) for the *New York Review of Sex*. We printed stickers and posters, of which this is one, 1970.

Brad Holland was the tireless talent in the Asylum. It was he who created the Press's colorful "Illustrated News of the Week" for the *East Village Other*, all lettered and color separated by hand, 1969.

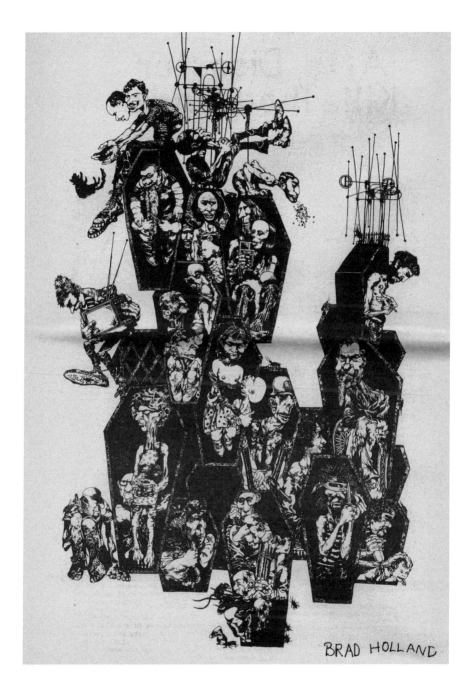

Brad Holland created this metaphoric Lower East Side tenement block composed of caskets as buildings (he put himself in one), 1972. He had tacked it up as a personal protest on the wall of Society of Illustrators NYC's only anti–Vietnam War art exhibition, where Brad's more formal work was also on display. It was summarily removed by the organizers.

New York Review of Sex & Politics, the *East Village Other*, *Screw*, and the *New York Ace*—and I was able to apply some of the lessons I learned from him to my jobs. For instance, I gave license to artists who sought to redefine their briefs so that personal solutions instead of conventional literal visualizations were possible.

By the early 1970s, before I came to the *New York Times*, Brad was already a fixture at its Op-Ed page and made such a mark that he was copied far and wide. The Op-Ed page was the most important illustration outlet in America, and he contributed illustrations that both complemented the articles and stood on their own as integral works of art. In 1974 I became the *Times* Op-Ed art director, and working with Brad was a great perk.

Over time we became equals, though I still get a bit irritable when I recall how tough he critiqued what I did. No one else exerted such a fundamental impact on the way I think about and practice in my field. Without Brad, I doubt if I would be doing what I do today. And without his fervency and passion for message art, American illustration would not be as conceptually astute as it is, but rather would still be locked between those old notions of sentimentality and romanticism.

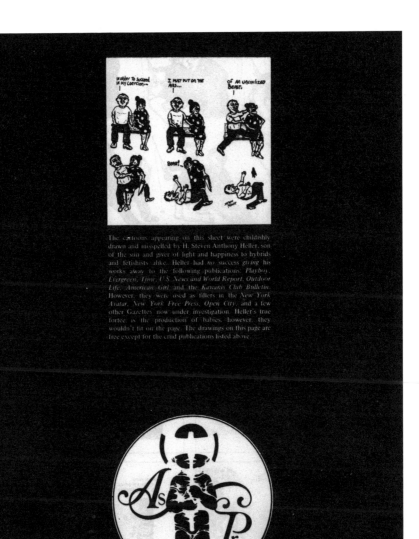

The Asylum Press

This is the flip side of my Asylum Press sample page (see page 87). Few, if any, of my drawings were selected by any of the papers our packet was mailed to.

A typical newsstand, probably on Eighth Street and Sixth Avenue in Greenwich Village in I969, where budding bohemians could buy any underground political or sex paper published in and outside New York. Photographer unknown.

CHAPTER 6

ℳl Goldstein, Pornosatirista

At age seventeen I was the first art director of *Screw*, the pioneering underground "sex review" that helped trigger the 1960s sexual revolution. It was cofounded by the outrageous Al Goldstein, who was also a trusted friend. For the better part of my subsequent career, in accordance with my dear grandma Ray's deathbed wish (she was never too happy with this episode in my career, although she did not berate me for it like my mom did), I've ostensibly tried to distance myself publicly from this dubious part of my past. But, in truth, I have used any flimsy excuse to tell my war stories from the porno-chic trenches.

I first met Al when he showed up at the *New York Free Press*, hawking a story he had written about being an industrial spy hired to steal secret documents. Although I illustrated the story for the cover of the *Freep*, I had little contact with him until he cooked up a scheme with Jim Buckley, the *Freep* managing editor and typesetter, to start the new sex paper. Al was hilariously funny and disarmingly ingratiating. We became immediate friends, the oddest of odd couples. He bragged about his "sex-capades" to me, and in him I confided my adolescent angst, for which he provided mostly useless but amusing advice.

In 2006, when the *New York Times Book Review* editors who had heard my *Screw* tales countless times asked me to review *I, Goldstein: My Screwed Life*, the autobiography by Al Goldstein with Josh Alan Friedman, I initially declined. Reason 1: Al and I had known each other for a long time, and a cardinal rule at the *Book Review* was never to review anyone you know well—friend or foe. Reason 2: I was convinced my wayward teenage exploits would be dredged up throughout his book, since not only was I present at *Screw*'s inception and other best-forgotten events but also I had also quit the magazine tearfully after fighting with Al about an inane logo he wanted me to use. I had then cofounded a short-lived competitor, the *New York Review of Sex & Politics*. It folded after twenty issues, prompting our distributor to claim I was the only person in New York who could make a sex paper fail. A few years later, I returned for a two-year stint at *Screw* (the health benefits and profit sharing were quite generous, and I received other unconventional perquisites that only a rascal like Al could conceive), at which time it achieved a high circulation and peak media attention—no doubt the result of my inventive art direction. Reason 3: After leaving *Screw* for the *Times* in 1974, I was subpoenaed as a hostile prosecution witness at Al's federal obscenity trial in Wichita, Kansas. My defiant testimony did not help the government's case. Al was acquitted.

I read *I, Goldstein* closely to see how I was represented, and to my utter bewilderment I was mentioned only twice, both times in the same short paragraph, along with two other art directors who also later moved to the *Times*. "Heller was so young," Al writes, "that, during one of our busts, he was thrown in juvenile lockup." I was busted not at *Screw* but at the *New York Review of Sex & Politics*. And I wasn't sent to juvenile lockup but placed in the adult lockup with the prostitutes.

Moreover, Al says not a word about my groundbreaking typography for *Screw*, nor about my designs for his other publications: *Mobster Times, Gadget, Smut, Smut from the Past, and Gay*. There is also nothing about how I hired the best illustrators from *Time, Newsweek*, and the *New York Times*, knowing they would give *Screw* some legitimacy. Nor any hint that I once asked Salvador Dalí to design an entire issue (he considered it for two weeks and then demurred, saying the $3,000 fee, the highest offered to any artist, was too low). *I, Goldstein* contains a photograph I believe I should be in—I vividly recall the shoot and everyone in it—but I'm not there. I'm guessing I wasn't airbrushed out, but rather that the published picture was taken when,

Gay, cover, February 1974. *Gay* was an offshoot of *Screw*'s regular column Homosexual Citizen. Art direction: World Domination Studio (which was me, with production by Ruth Rock). An editor's note indicated that Truman Capote was scheduled to write an article but "took ill and withdrew from the assignment" just as the issue was ready for press.

Gay, cover, 1973. *Screw*'s Al Goldstein and Jim Buckley were listed on the masthead as Wizards. Pictures of Bette Midler (here at the 1973 Gay Pride rally) were the most frequently published photos in the magazine. Photographer: Eric Scott Jacobs.

Gay, contents pages, nos. 106 (no month given, 1973) and 111 (February 1974).
I designed many such pages for *Screw*'s offshoot magazines using the innovative
Milton Glaser–designed *New York Magazine* contents format, with small
highlight/reference photos and large page numbers.

for a split second, I left the room. Well, that was the final insult! Realizing my credibility would forever be challenged at the *New York Times Book Review* office, I accepted the review assignment—if only to set the record straight.

Yet aside from the humiliation of being all but erased from the story, given my firsthand knowledge of everything from the founding (I was there when *Screw* was conceived, during a meeting at the *New York Free Press*) to the birth of Al's to-be-estranged son, Jordan (I was outside the delivery room), I can attest that the record is set forth faithfully, for the most part, and also entertainingly. In fact, Al's life and legacy deserves even fuller analysis to truly establish what, besides dirty words and deeds, he has contributed to American pop culture, and in particular to the cause of free sexual speech and mores.

While Al has been vilified, satirized, and marginalized over the years, he has was one of America's more complex and interesting outlaws. His brushes with the law on First Amendment issues are legendary and significant. Even though he never had a case tried before the US Supreme Court, he deserves at least the same cinematic treatment as Larry Flynt, the publisher of *Hustler*—a magazine that Al, in his telling, inadvertently sponsored, since Flynt repeatedly "poached my editors over the years." (Then again, Al writes, "I have always considered my employees to be like Kleenex—meant to be used and discarded.") Flynt had his Hollywood moment: after winning a free-speech case before the Supreme Court, which stemmed from a legal altercation with Reverend Jerry Falwell and getting shot and paralyzed by a would-be assassin, he earned himself a critically acclaimed 1996 biopic directed by Miloš Forman. That same year Al, who has consistently played second fiddle to lesser outlaws, was the subject of a mediocre documentary, *Screwed: Al Goldstein's Kingdom of Porn*.

Yet when Al and Jim founded *Screw*, nothing—not Hugh Hefner's *Playboy* or Ralph Ginzburg's *Eros* or Barney Rosset's *Evergreen Review*—had yet come close to addressing sex with such unvarnished candor and biting wit. Al was an equal opportunity exploiter of men, women, and art directors, but his raunchy humor raised the bar for porn from socially unredeemable smut to ironic social commentary. Sure, *Screw* was shocking, offensive, and downright obscene—but as the motto on its early covers announced, it was "Best in the Field It Created."

Before conceiving *Screw*, Al worked for gossip columnist Walter Winchell, a photographer for the Fair Play for Cuba Committee (he was once jailed in Havana), and a press photographer for Pakistan International Airlines (he accompanied Jackie Kennedy on her goodwill tour of Pakistan in 1962). He was also employed by Myron Fass, the tabloid publisher of the "blood and guts" men's magazines *Hush-Hush News* and the *National Mirror*. (Al used his friends' names for characters in stories with gory headlines such as "Lover Shoves Icepick Up Lover's Nose.") As a respite from this sordid journalism, he sold the *New York Free Press* his guilt-ridden confessions of being an industrial spy for the Bendix Corporation, which I illustrated as a cover story.

The *Freep*, July 4, 1968. My first cover illustration was for an article by Al Goldstein.

Al often railed about having to write such unremittingly gratuitous violence while sex, which his editors called "unmentionable acts," remained taboo. He deemed his employers "bottom-feeders" and decided to start a publication along the lines of *Consumer Reports* that would "detail sex, but never violence." He was also eager to experience his fair share of those unmentionable acts. And so, in 1968, *Screw* was born.

At the time, social and political underground papers, like New York's *East Village Other*, were making considerable income from personal ads. The *Freep*, as I recall, sold best when seminude women were featured on its cover, even if the rest of issue was devoted to, say, the rioting at the 1968 Democratic National Convention. The first issue of *Screw* I designed (if one can call it that, since I had no idea what I was doing) was a ragtag assemblage of typo-filled articles and stock photographs of simulated carnal congress. It also included Homosexual Citizen (to my knowledge the first gay-themed column published in a heterosexual magazine); Al's regular porno movie review column,

Screw, cover, December 1968. Art director: Steven Heller. Photographer: Al Goldstein.

with its unorthodox rating system (the Peter Meter); and the mildly pornographic comic strip I drew and named after my NYU philosophy teacher. The first issue's cover showed a fairly plain, decidedly unerotic woman kneeling in a two-piece bathing suit, fetchingly holding a very long kosher salami. As an afterthought, we slapped a warning label on a corner of the picture.

Al and his partner Jim hand-distributed the copies, which were surreptitiously printed at night in Brooklyn, and then waited for the shit to hit the fan. *Screw* led to their own frequent arrests and one unintended outcome: blind newsdealers (New York City had many) were jailed for selling pornography. Al, who leaned politically to the left, promptly used this harassment as a First Amendment issue and turned *Screw* into his soapbox against censorship. Those of us who worked for him were convinced we were fighting for a transcendent cause. It was the sixties, after all.

Al was the archetypal pornographer—bloated, goateed, cigar chomping, apparently eczema-ridden—and a counterintuitive friend to me. But he also saw himself as belonging to a distinguished line of outlaws, including Lenny Bruce and Henry Miller, whom he proudly interviewed in *Screw*. He also attracted the likes of writers Gay Talese (who wrote about him in *Thy Neighbor's Wife*), Philip Roth (whose alter ego Nathan Zuckerman impersonates a Goldstein-type figure in *The Anatomy Lesson*), and Jerzy Kosinski (who, Al reports, accompanied him to New York swingers' club Plato's Retreat for a night of debauchery). He also hobnobbed with the stars who submitted to the *Screw* interview. He had a high-priced psychiatrist, Theodore Isaac Rubin, and a prestigious constitutional lawyer, Herald Price Fahringer (who was my lawyer first). He even befriended one

Screw, cover, February 1969. Photographer: Al Goldstein. My final issue. (I did not design the psychedelic logo.)

Screw, cover, July 1969. With a redrawn psychedelic logo. Art directors: Brill & Waldstein. Stock photograph.

of his ideological enemies, the conservative legal scholar Ernest van den Haag (who testified against Al in his first trial).

Al, in addition to being a porn king, made an art of self-loathing. Despite his aggressively funny writing style, he doubted he was truly intelligent. A self-described "bed-wetting stutterer from Brooklyn" and a punching bag for neighborhood toughs in his youth, he feared he would become a milquetoast like his father, a photojournalist who exhibited courage in World War II but addressed elevator operators as "sir." (He later toiled in *Screw*'s mailroom.) Al, forever self-conscious about his weight, compensated by making voraciousness the cornerstone of his identity. He describes, touchingly, how as a teenager he was treated by a diet doctor—with whom, it turned out, his mother was having an affair because "my father was so inadequate." Thus, he entered manhood primed to defy all who crossed him, and he fulfilled this wish, metaphorically flushing hypocrites and incompetents from President Richard Nixon to his auto mechanic in a ceremonial toilet bowl on his weekly Shit List.

Screw, interior feature spread, February 1969. Typical of Al Goldstein's bathroom humor (or perhaps it was my idea?); anyway, it was published in my last issue before starting the *New York Review of Sex*.

Above all, Al really wanted to be somebody. His memoir chronicles the improbable rise of a guy who each year renewed his taxi license just in case he hit the skids, and who was deeply in debt (his Jane Street apartment was stuffed with electronic gadgets bought on credit) but later owned a townhouse in Manhattan, a mansion in Florida, cars with drivers, and millions of dollars' worth of watches. Then came his spiraling downfall: the costly lawsuits, criminal battles, and divorces. *Screw* went out of business in 2003. "Marshals were summoned for nonpayment of rent," Al noted. A year before he died, Al was convicted of harassing a former employee and sent to jail on Rikers Island, where he became gravely ill. He lost his entire fortune.

He was homeless, living on the street. Toward the end of his life, he resided in Staten Island in an apartment paid for by the comedian and magician Penn Jillette. The one-time pariah, the host of the pioneering cable TV show *Midnight Blue*, wandered the Manhattan streets: a porn king without a crown, throne, or *Screw*.

Al was never as presentable or culturally palatable as Hugh Hefner, and *Screw* was never a beautiful and expensive production like *Playboy*. But had Al Goldstein not dared to create his sex review, the floodgates of a more expansive and liberating publishing culture might never have

Goldstein announces my leaving my second stint with *Screw* for the Op-Ed page of the *New York Times*, October 1974. Illustrator: Yossarian.

opened. As for me, had I not been *Screw*'s art director and been given the freedom and encouragement to learn my craft, I would not have gotten my job at the *New York Times*.

A New Column By Lyle Stuart, P. 16
Swingtime In Paris, P. 6   Long Distance Lust, P. 8

SCREW

50 CENTS   THE SEX REVIEW   NUMBER 166

WARNING: Sexual material of an adult nature. This literature is not intended for minors and under no circumstances are they to view it, possess it, or place orders for the merchandise offered herein.

Screw, cover, May 2, 1972. Milton Glaser redesigned the magazine starting with number 138, October 25, 1971, including the logo with the upturned *E* (for erection). Illustrator: Tom Hachtman.

Screw, cover, July 17, 1972. This was one of my favorite covers, blending savvy and nostalgia in a witty parody of 1930s Fleischer Studios animation. Illustrator: Leslie Cabarga.

Screw, cover, August 7, 1972. Another parody of the Fleischer Studios'
style and their star character, Betty Boop. Illustrator: Leslie Cabarga.

108

Screw, cover, January 8, 1973. Surrealism was long associated with eroticism.
I frequently used artists who worked in this manner that tickled reader's imagination.
Illustrator: Philippe Weisbecker.

Screw, cover, February 26, 1973. Sometimes I would use a photograph
if it had a special illustrative quality. Photographer: Jon Stevens.

JON STEVENS
SHINING SEX OBJECTS

TEXT BY
DEAN LATIMER

Photograph: Caren Golden

The first thing a lot of people are going to ask, when you tell them of all the silver-painted naked people you saw in SCREW this week, is this: "If the people were really naked, then how did they avoid the doubloon-sized patch of bare flesh needed to provide the epidermis with a sufficient respiration surface, in order to avoid asphyxiation?" That old promo hype from the hustlers of *Goldfinger,* who unleashed a rumor to the effect that a budding starlet perished of suffocation from being electroplated with 14K gilt over her entire squirming body-surface, is still current, and for some reason people still cling to it, even when presented with Jon Stevens' "art studies" of Catherine May and her chums cavorting about dipped in silver from head to toe.

"It's just a silver paint solution on a baby oil base," explains Stevens impatiently, hot to move on to a discussion of the deeper aesthetic significance of his work. "It's applied with a sponge by the model herself, or himself; it helps them relax, get in touch with their sensuality. You'll notice the study of Catherine here, with one hand between her thighs. She was extremely well-attuned to her flesh that day, a feeling I managed to capture after letting her move about for a while with the paint sliding against her skin . . ." Stevens just set up the lights around her, warmed the strobe, and started flashing away. Later on, the guys in the photo-lab printed her up on special heat-sensitive paper; and the highly edifying —not to mention edible—result you may behold in this spread.

In fact, had you only known, all last month you could have beheld the same silver lady in the pages of *Gallery* magazine, the new one that looks just like *Playboy.* "I was getting so impatient haggling with *Playboy* and *Penthouse* for money," affirms Stevens, "that when *Gallery* promised to pay out front, I jumped for it. I really needed the money fast."

Silver Strokes for Silver Folks

Screw, interior feature page, February 26, 1973. Herb Lubalin's very tight typesetting was my major typography inspiration.

III

Screw, cover, December 10, 1973, was a hilarious political satire referring to the infamous missing portions of President Richard Nixon's White House tape recordings. Illustrator: Edward Sorel.

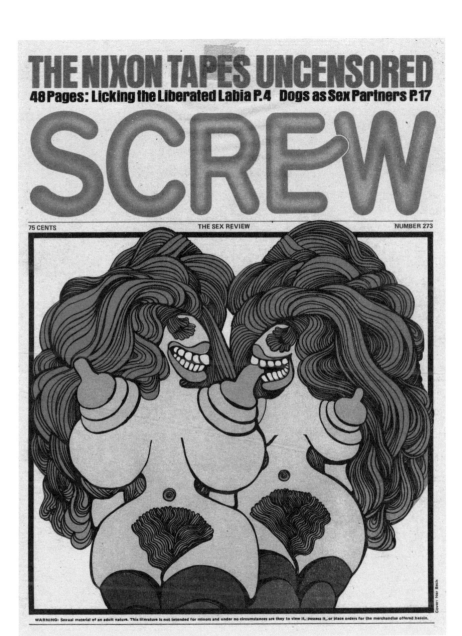

Screw, cover, May 27, 1974. I was very taken by abstract Eastern European comic posters, which were slightly less heavy-handed than American comics. Illustrator: Ner Beck.

Screw, covers, February 25, 1974 (top); September 30, 1974 (bottom).
Marshall Arisman expelled me from SVA, and I gave him cover assignments in return.
His nightmarish aesthetic appealed to me, but not to *Screw*'s average horny readers.

Edited by Michael Perkins
Designed by Steve Heller
Brought to you by the wonderful
guys who bring you Screw
(The Sex Review)
Jim Buckley and Al Goldstein.
Cover Painting: Mike Kanarek

Smut From the Past, front/back covers (top); credit and contents pages (bottom),
circa 1973. This biannual romp through vintage pinup and spicy photographs allowed me
to design in any nostalgic manner. Designer: Steven Heller. Illustrator: Mike Kanarek.

CHAPTER 7

Brush with Genius

My work gave me great opportunities to meet a slew of curiously notable sixties characters, including one who has since earned fame and fortune, much to my amazement. Yayoi Kusama is an art world luminary known for her esoteric soft sculptures, immersive happenings, and obsessive polka dot experiences. She became one of Japan's most internationally revered living artists. With art that strides the abstract and bizarre, this orange-wigged living doll is the consummate avant-gardist. She resides in a self-contained bubble of spacey illusions and ephemeral visions, and for almost five decades has lived voluntarily in a Tokyo psychiatric hospital across the street from her painting studio. Frequent exhibitions at MoMA, the Whitney Museum of American Art, and the Tate Modern; prestigious gallery shows; mountains of published monographs; a graphic novel/biography; and dozens of products bearing her imprimatur attest to her colossal global appeal.

I met Yayoi in 1968. I had no idea she was part of Fluxus art scenes; to me she was merely an eccentric du jour, one of many the sixties had given rise to—a kook among kooks, a narcissist among narcissists. I was the rookie art director of *Screw*, and I fielded almost daily phone calls from

(Left) *New York Free Press*, cover, November 1968. We found that the paper always did better on the newsstand with nude pictures. "Happening" artist Yayoi Kusama provided us with many photographs from her events.

(Below) *Screw*, interior page, February 7, 1969. This photograph was taken at one of Yayoi Kusama's happenings. The potato-like soft sculptures and polka dots were her signature conceits.

···GEORGIE AT THE ORGY···········

couples sitting around. Looks like just another party, doesn't it? The big difference is that blonde at the end of the sofa—the one with the big tits?—the thought that just a little while she'll be wrapping those lovely legs around you is enough to start the juices flowing.

The doorbell rings and you crane your neck to see what kind of action is about to enter your life. How does a guy have the balls to bring a barracuda like that? No tits, bad skin and probably a screamer!

That's one of the chances you take when you go to a swing. You walk in with a really groovy chick who's got all it takes to give these schmucks a night they'll talk about for the rest of the year, and you wind up with a broad who'd probably pay you to go down on her. This used to happen to a friend of mine all the time. "I come in with a sirloin steak," he used to say, "and all I see is hamburger."

One of the world's funniest sights is a chick at her first swing. She's thought about it all week long and mentally, she's fought the good fight. She's thought it through and convinced herself that there's not a reason in the world why she can't really dig this scene. She loves to ball . . . she digs being eaten . . . she thinks people that are hung up sexually are just weak souls that society has crippled.

But now she's here—face to face with the real thing. Her eyes dart around the room endlessly and you can almost read her thoughts: "If that guy comes near me, I'll kick him in the balls . . . oh, my God, I went to school with that one—she's a dyke!—oh, yeah, he's gay—I think he's got a hard-on already—I'd love to feel his tongue between my tits . . ."

When the action begins, she usually holds on to her date for dear life. Most often, a broad is turned on or off almost immediately—so it makes a great deal of difference what the crowd looks like on her first night.

The most annoying thing at a swing is "the miser," Usually, it's a stupid looking putz with a good looking head. He holds on to her all night. Doesn't want her to ball with anyone.

Why did he bring her? He could have balled her at his pad. Just to ruin my evening, that's why he brought her, that bastard. Actually, most of these creeps only enjoy balling if someone is watching.

People always ask: All right, you're sitting around drinking and smoking and laughing and talking—how does the action start? Nine times out of ten, some broad will get up and say something like: "Hey, what are we waiting time for? Let's do what we came her to do . . ."

And so it begins. The grab bag. The ones that looked so promising in the beginning turn out to be the biggest bombs. The ones that started out like a tea party turn into New Year's Eve. Sometimes the door will open in the middle of a bad scene and three groovy broads will make you glad you didn't leave ten minutes ago.

If you dig it right, it can be the grooviest scene going. Like somebody pulled a curtain on the square world outside. Fucking and sucking in a sweet, timeless void. The incredible chain—the feel of a wild tongue on your cock while you're eating a broad who's turning another broad on.

And now it's over. Don't feel bad 'cause you shot your load with the wrong broad. And that ugly broad really turned out to be a screamer,

too. "Noisiest come in the east," some guy called her. The one with the nice tits is comin' over to wash off your cock with a damp cloth. "Where were you all night," she asks. "I was dyin' to fuck you."

You like her? She's here with her husband—the schmuck with the beard who only likes to watch. Don't ask for her number—that's another unwritten law of the swing. But I'll make sure they're at my place on Friday night. You gonna try to make it? O.K.—but do me a favor, show up with your own broad. You bet your ass they're not easy to find. You'll be makin' phone calls all week long.

PORNO PALS

ONE EARLY MORNING IN MAY THE GANG DROPPED IN ON ALICE IN NEW YORK'S

CENTRAL PARK. "YOU'RE LATE," SAID THE RABBIT AS HE SCRATCHED HIS BALLS. THE MAD HATTER WAS ONE UP ON THE GROUP THOUGH AND

[nut is euphemism for head]. SELF-OBLITERATION BY KUSAMA ... LANGUAGE BY BUCKLEY

PLACED A WELL-LAID SCREW ON THE MOUSE'S TAIL. "GOTCHA BY THE TAIL" WALLOWED THE HATTER AS ALICE   KICKED HIM ON THE NUT

Screw, center spread, November 1968. Yayoi Kusama orchestrated her art happenings in public spaces. This one, which she shot in Central Park, worked perfectly as a spread. Yayoi was very pleased.

Yayoi aggressively hawking photographs of the orgiastic happenings she had choreographed throughout New York City. She was the inexhaustible obsessive orchestrator of throngs of naked hippies, some wearing masks of President Richard Nixon and FBI director J. Edgar Hoover, among other bêtes noires of the era, while covered in polka dots and scampering through undulating piles of potato-shaped phallic soft sculptures. On one occasion she and her cohorts occupied the *Alice in Wonderland* monument in Central Park for a photo that I published as a centerspread in the *New York Review of Sex & Politics*. Yayoi routinely appeared in these photographs as ringmaster, wearing a polka-dotted leotard. She also published her own tabloid, *Kusama Presents an Orgy: Nudity, Love, Sex & Beauty for Adults Over 21*. Al Goldstein assigned me to be her conduit to him.

Her phone calls were annoyingly routine. "I come now, bring photos," Yayoi announced in such a fast, clipped, heavily accented English, I almost believed that she was speaking, and I was understanding, Japanese. Moments later, as though she had been in a phone booth down the street, she'd arrive at the door bearing a stack of poorly printed black-and-white prints. Usually, she'd stay for an hour or so, explaining the hidden meanings of every single shot. Listening to her was torture.

I'd never met anyone as self-promotional as Yayoi. But like in Woody Allen's joke about the guy who had a brother who thought he was a chicken and, when asked why he wasn't committed to a mental asylum, said, "Because we need the eggs!"—well, at *Screw* we needed her photos. Yayoi kept the underground sex press well stocked—and as I recall, her photos, unlike those from most stock porn pic suppliers, were free.

A 2010 blog post in which I mentioned Yayoi's hijinks brought me to the attention of Heather Lenz, who was filming a documentary about the artist. A seven-minute version, titled *Kusama: Princess of Polka Dots*, was cut for Yayoi's Tate Modern exhibit. I was surprised to learn that this person whom I had reduced to a blip in the corner of my memory had become such a renowned artist—said to be the most widely sold female artist in the world. If only I had saved those files full of prints, I might be rich.

Heather was introduced to Yayoi's work in the early nineties. She was studying for degrees in art history and fine arts at the time, and her textbooks seldom contained any mention of women artists. "Then one day, a sculpture professor showed me a photo of Yayoi's sculptures," she told me in an interview. "It was love at first sight."

Some years later Heather decided to make a film about Yayoi. First she conceived it as a biopic, but later she decided a documentary was a better fit: "It would be more interesting to have Ms. Kusama tell her story in her own words while she was still alive, and while that was still an option." Heather is now an expert on Yayoi's life as a struggling artist in New York during the sixties.

By the time I met Yayoi in 1968, "her work had already taken many forms," Heather told me. Her early works included small paintings made from ink and watercolor on paper. When she moved to New York in 1958 she started making larger paintings on canvas. Then she began making sculpture, then installations that included her sculpture, paintings, and other elements, such as mirrors and macaroni (which in some cases, covered gallery floors and required guests to walk over the crunchy pieces of dried pasta). Then she moved onto the happenings she was conceiving when she became our ad hoc photo supplier. "During that era, she also made 'orgy clothes,' with strategically cut holes," Heather added. Then, after moving back to Japan in the seventies, Yayoi made collages and wrote semi-autobiographical novels and poems. Since then, she has made paintings, sculptures, installations, and a variety of objects, including furniture, purses, puzzles, stickers, and limited-edition phones shaped liked dogs.

"Respect for Ms. Kusama's work has increased dramatically in recent years," Heather said about the first woman to represent Japan at the prestigious Venice Biennale in 1993. "Like many artists who are ahead of their time, she was misunderstood in her hometown for decades. But now there is a museum there with the largest permanent collection of her art."

Heather posited that part of what makes Yayoi so compelling is that she was willing to go to great lengths to pursue her passion to make art. "I think a lot of the art she created in the sixties was really ahead of its time, and that makes it important," she says. "Personally, though, I'll always have a soft spot for the collages she produced in Japan after returning there."

Heather Lenz's film was released as *Kusama Infinity: The Life and Art of Yayoi Kusama*. My interview was cut from the film, my insights were minimal, but I was grateful to reappreciate the artist whom I considered as simply crazy.

Working for the *Freep* and *EVO* brought me in contact with the New York City police department's undercover "Red Squad." Here, reporter Ray Schultz and I attempted to chat with a detective known as Captain Finnegan. Photographer: Joseph Stevens.

CHAPTER 8

Growing Up Underground

During the day, I worked as art director of *Screw*, but two or three nights a week, I made layouts at the *East Village Other* (*EVO*).

Art critic Robert Hughes once described the weekly paste-up night at *EVO* as "a Dada experience." The year was 1970, and none of us who were toiling into the wee hours of the morning at one of America's oldest (founded in 1965) hippie underground papers knew what Hughes, a savvy young Australian writer and historian, was talking about. Nevertheless, we all assumed that to get *Time* magazine's newly appointed art critic to spend some of his first weeknights in America with us, we were doing something weird and perhaps even important. "Dada was the German anti-art political-art movement of the 1920s," he explained in his twangy Aussie accent. "And this is the closest thing I've come to seeing it recreated today. I'm really grateful for the chance to be here."

He needn't have been so grateful. He was as welcome as any other artist, writer, musician, and sundry local habitué at that time. The East Village was populated with avant-gardists galore, all testing the limits of countercultural tolerance. Detective Frank Serpico (played by Al Pacino in the eponymous 1973 biopic), the most famous whistle-blowing cop in America at the time, was briefly stationed at the local Ninth Precinct and would come around periodically in his various undercover costumes to schmooze with *EVO* staffers. Paste-up night was open to anybody who drifted up to the dark, creaky loft above Bill Graham's Fillmore East, a former Loews Theatre turned rock palace on Second Avenue and Sixth Street, next door to Ratner's Dairy Restaurant (where my first wedding reception was held), in a neighborhood that in the early 1900s was the heart of New York's Yiddish Theater. In the 1960s, it was the East Coast's hippie capital.

Beginning at seven or eight o'clock at night and lasting at least until dawn, the regular and transient layout staffs took the jumble of counter-culture journalism and antiestablishment screeds that was the paper's editorial meat and threw it helter-skelter onto layouts that were pretty anarchic. Anyone, whether they had graphic design experience or not, could join in, yet many of the gadfly layout artists were too stoned to complete their pages, which were finished by the *EVO* art staff on the long subway ride to the offset printer in the bowels of Brooklyn.

EVO's paste-up was a tribal ritual. Every Thursday night for well over a year I joined the others in the group encounter that was part makeup and part make-out session (plenty of hippie chicks were part of the cast of characters). I had done all-nighters before, but none were as fever-pitched or as drug-stimulated as *EVO*. While I harbored superstitions about drugs and never touched the stuff myself, joints and acid tabs were payment for a good night's work. Someone routinely emerged from the editor's office around 8:30 p.m. with a shoebox full of the stuff, as well as with the night's layout

RAT, cover, June 1968. This image borrows from Russian revolutionary posters. Illustrator unknown.

assignments, which included at least three pages of "intimate" classifieds. The layout crew would help themselves to grass (the acid was saved until after the session was over) and manuscripts, find their tables, select their decorative ruling tapes and transfer-type sheets, and settle down to "design" pages.

The editor's office, where everyone congregated at one time or another during the night, was a dimly lit cubicle papered with manuscripts, clippings, proofs, and other underground papers. It was also where *EVO*'s editor, Yakov Cohen, who suffered from a degenerative nerve disease, spent most of his time. There he schmoozed with ten to fifteen habitués while snorting his drug of choice, cocaine, which gave him cavernous nostrils, the

EVO staff during Christmas party (circa 1973); I am on the right. Photographer: Joseph Stevens.

focal point of his yellow-tinged, hollowed-out face. Beginning early every Thursday morning, however, this was also where—in solitude—he would read the week's copy and as diligently as possible put the finishing touches on manuscripts submitted by his staff of serious writers and columnists. Yet his mastery of the blue pencil was minimal at best, and by any measure the manuscripts remained unfinished even after his editing. In fact, the only way to ensure clean copy, if one really cared about such trifles, was to edit it oneself.

Way back in 1965, as a fifteen year old, I was an early *EVO*tee. I had stumbled upon one of the first issues at a newsstand. The cover, which I remember vividly, had a photo collage of a serpent emerging from battle fatigues worn by America's commanding general in Vietnam, William Westmoreland. Haunting is not a strong enough word to describe the impact that this had on a teen just a year or two out of Valley Forge Military Academy summer

New York Avatar, cover, July 6, 1968. The magazine published some of my
first drawings, but this cover was not mine. Illustrator: Eben Given.

school, where, surprisingly, I had learned about the military impossibility of winning the Vietnam War. I savored each *EVO* issue, as when I was an adolescent boy I would covet my contraband copy of *Playboy*. I made a visit to *EVO*'s original storefront office on Tompkins Square Park to inquire whether they could use volunteer labor. I was met at the door by one of the founding editors, Walter Bowart, who said, "Come back, kid, when you're not jailbait." Though my pride was hurt, I continued to venture into the East Village after school in the hope that I would earn my stripes as a hippie first class and then, despite being underage, be invited back into *EVO*'s inner sanctum.

The road to *EVO* was long and circuitous. Before I could be invited in, I had to make myself valuable. So, I turned to making cartoons of angst-ridden little men with long hair and mustaches without genitalia in situations that were religious in nature but with a touch of Jules Feiffer's irony. The *Village Voice*'s Feiffer was my hero, but the inspiration for this subject matter came from Mr. Deme at the McBurney School, who, as mentioned before, had my head shaved by a sadistic barber.

When I moved on to the progressive Walden School, where I was allowed to have long hair and a clip-on earring, I began hawking my artwork to the other New York undergrounds that had begun around 1967. I found a receptive outlet at the *New York Avatar*, the journal of the Boston cult leader and jugband musician Mel Lyman. I was taken under the wing of its art director, Don Lewis— a gaunt, demonic, Charles Manson doppelganger—who taught me the virtue of fanning out lines of type and other underground-layout tricks. *Avatar* was ostensibly concerned with the creepy

Bitch, cover, 1974. Art director: Steven Heller. Photographer uncredited.

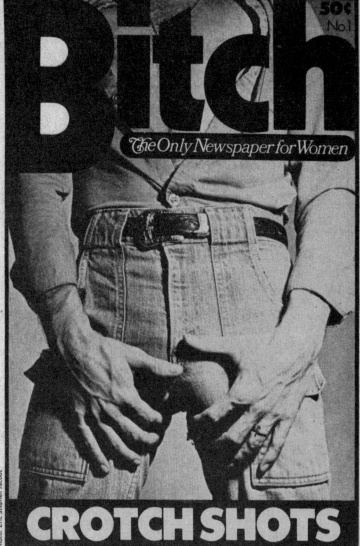

Blowjob Symposium
Is Jackie Kennedy Really a Woperone?

Bitch

50¢
No.1

The Only Newspaper for Women

Photo: Eric Stephen Jacobs

CROTCH SHOTS

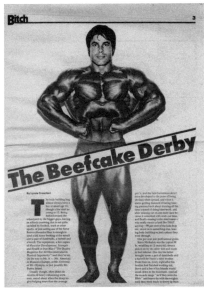

(Opposite) *Bitch*, cover, February 1974. Photographer: Eric Stephen Jacobs. (Above) Contents and feature pages from *Bitch*, April 1974. Art director and designer: Steven Heller.

New York Ace, cover, March 15, 1972. This latter-day underground attempted to replace the *East Village Other*, with many of the same staff. Art director: Steven Heller. Illustrator: Jay Kinney.

machinations of Lyman's consciousness and subconsciousness and their effect on his followers. My drawings of Christlike characters fit nicely into his agenda/brand.

Later I found a temporary haven at the *Rat*, a Students for a Democratic Society (SDS)–oriented tabloid. I produced two comic strips for *Rat* that dealt, rather simplistically, with issues of racism and inequality. *Rat* editors mistakenly saw in me a future Ron Cobb, the brilliant political cartoonist of the *Los Angeles Free Press*. But after publishing the first two I couldn't come up with any other socially satiric strips, and I was dropped.

Finally, as earlier mentioned, I lucked into a comparatively full-time job as a paste-up artist, cartoonist, and, two weeks later, art director of the *New York Free Press*. There I learned a few rights and many wrongs of newspaper design. The *Freep* was rather conventional. Its columns were standard; its typesetting was usually justified.

EVO, on the other hand, was resolutely formless. While it had an anchored editorial page, its features and columns were not constricted by either aesthetic or functional rules. By the time I arrived at *EVO* in 1970, five years after its founding and two after its heyday, the layout staff

New York Ace, interior page, February 15, 1972. Article on Bob Dylan's Hebrew teacher, known as "One-Legged Terry."
Illustrator: Yossarian.

of between five and ten on any given Thursday comprised rank amateurs without a clue how to create consistent design, even if they wanted to. I, on the other hand, was now a two-year veteran learned in the ways of the grid and central axis composition, and I knew the right way to refer to a magazine (or newspaper), as a "book."

During the first couple of weeks of working at *EVO*, I created islands of misbegotten elegance in a sea of appropriate ugliness. But I became bored, indeed envious, of the naïfs around me. The biggest influence on

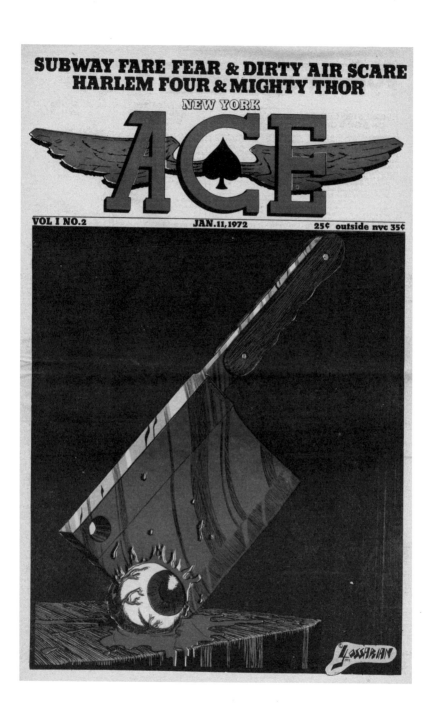

New York Ace, cover, January II, 1972. The cover symbolism symbolically smashes the *East Village Other* eye logo. Illustrator: Yossarian.

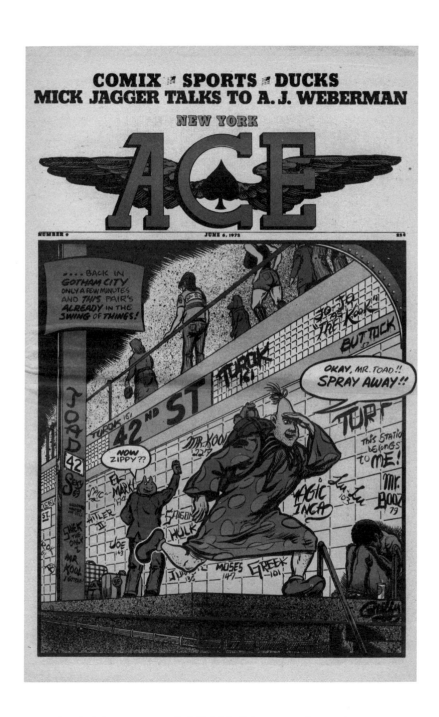

New York Ace, cover, June 6, 1972. Bill Griffith introduces his popular comix character, Zippy the Pinhead. Art director: Steven Heller.

New York Ace, cover, February 20, 1972: "N.Y. is Fear City."
Art director and cover designer: Steven Heller.

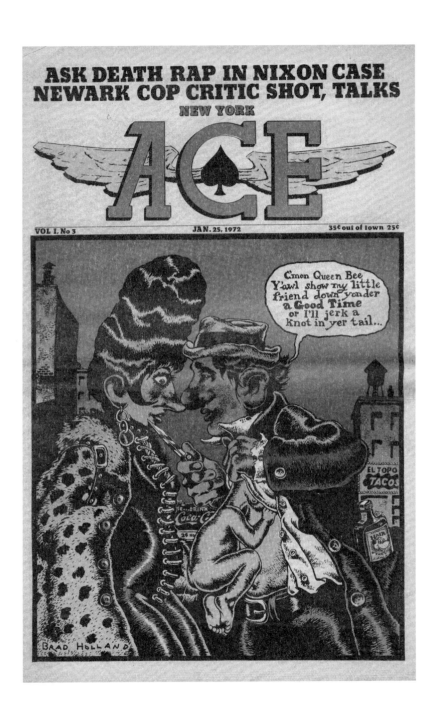

New York Ace, cover, January 25, 1972. Brad Holland could do whatever he wanted in the paper. Art director: Steven Heller.

New York Ace, cover, March 1972: "The Advent of Spring." Art director:
Steven Heller. Illustrator: Skeeter Grant (aka Art Spiegelman).

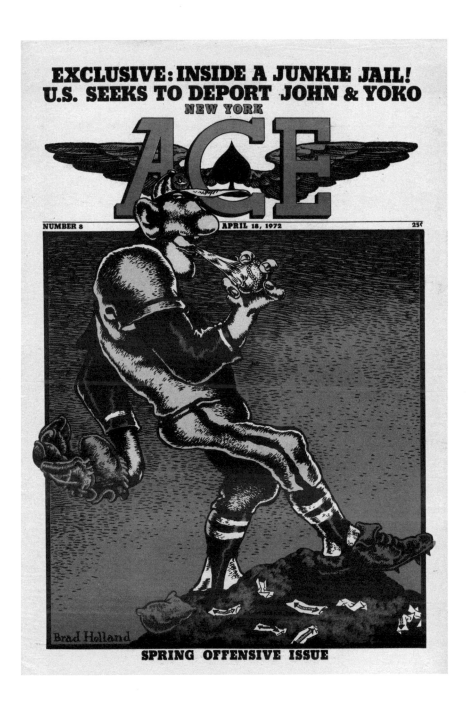

New York Ace, cover, April 18, 1972. Baseball season begins, and so, too, street protests and rallies. Art director: Steven Heller. Illustrator: Brad Holland.

137

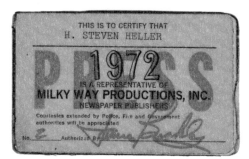

Press passes for the *New York Free Press*, 1968, and Milky Way Productions (publisher of *Screw* and its offshoots), 1972. With the *Freep* card I could get into the Fillmore East for free to see any rock concert.

me in those sessions, however, was watching veteran animator and coke connoisseur, Fred Mogubgub, draw obsessively intricate designs for covers (including the masthead) and inside pages that were often printed in a split fountain, going from unreadable yellow to brilliant orange to faint green. Fred was a pioneer commercial animator with a quirky, rough, but detailed comic style that changed the look of animated commercials in the early 1960s. When I was a kid, I marveled at his hilarious 7 Up bottles that can-canned across my TV screen.

I began to play with copy by blowing up words and laying down heavy ruling tape over or under copy blocks to emphasize key passages. I integrated various found and clipped images around text and headlines to further invigorate the page. Soon my *EVO* layouts were as ugly (or vibrant) as the others and still had the semblance of readable text. The pages became textures. I likened my work to literally letting my hair down, which I wore in a tight ponytail.

By 1972 *EVO*'s circulation, which is reported to have once been around seventy-five thousand nationwide, had plummeted to five or six thousand, and most of that was for the sex ads and classifieds that it took to stay afloat. This was consistent with the demise of the underground press in general, which either evolved into mainstream alternative journalism or just died. Some of *EVO*'s elite went on to the *SoHo Weekly News*, which sought respectability but never attained the circulation figures. Other *EVO*tees went on to other publishing ventures, and some simply disappeared.

The issues of *EVO* printed on cheap newsprint are hard to find these days, either because they were thrown away or turned to dust. Those that remain in the hands of collectors, however, represent a remarkable period of counterculture publishing, naïf design, and youthful exuberance that marked one of the most democratic periods in American history, when the means of cheap communication was in the hands of many.

For me, I learned how much fun it was to make ad hoc design. While I have continued a rather reserved course with my art direction, my *EVO* experience was not a youthful fling, but a point of departure. Thanks to Robert Hughes, I started to study the history of Dada, and, in that spirit, I decided that every designer needed a Dada period, if only to clear one's head of the rules and strictures of design. Like a decongestant, *EVO* cleared my head.

NEW YORK FREE PRESS
and high school free press
NEW YEARS BENEFIT,
JANUARY *8, 1968, 8 P.M
at FILLMORE EAST"
*NORMAN MAILER,
CHARLIE MINGUS,
THE FUGS and many many
more, details on back page.*

NEW YORK FREE PRESS

Second Class Postage Paid at New York, N.Y.

15 CENTS

Dec. 29, 1968   Jan. 9, 1969
Vol. I No. 51 & 52

OUT OF TOWN:
25 Cents

FREE PRESS PHOTO BY HAP STEWART

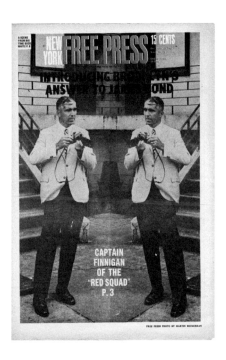

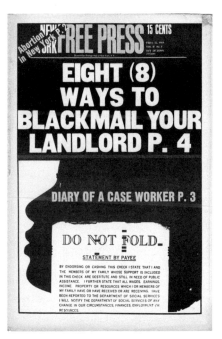

(Opposite): *New York Free Press*, cover, December 29, 1968. This issue sold well, for obvious reasons. Art director: Steven Heller. Photographer: Hap Stewart.
(Left) *New York Free Press*, cover, December 29, 1968. Captain Finnegan of the Red Squad caught photographing demonstrators at Vietnam War protest rally. Art director: Steven Heller. (Right) *New York Free Press*, cover, February 6, 1969. At its journalistic best the paper covered topical, hot-button issues in the city. Art director: Steven Heller.

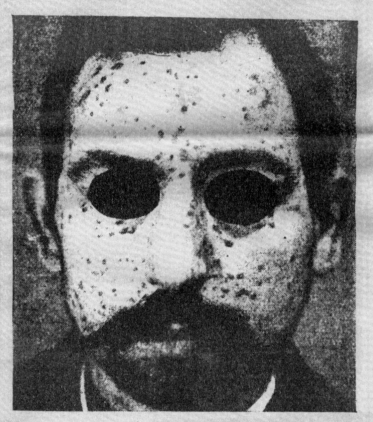

leary panthers mogubgub

THE east village OTHER

vol.5 no.51   nov.17,1970   25¢ncnyc   35¢outside

(Above) *East Village Other*, cover, November 17, 1970. Designer: Charlie Frick.
(Opposite) Back cover. Illustrator: Fred Mogubgub.

143

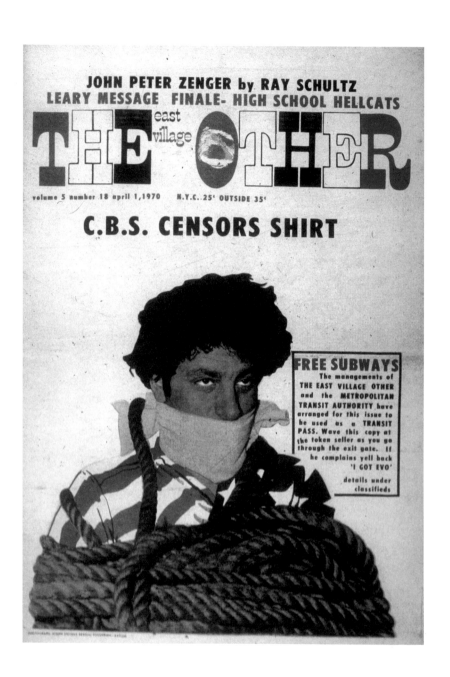

East Village Other, cover, April I, 1970. Abbie Hoffman was a frequent visitor to *EVO*'s office. He was arrested for wearing an American flag shirt to Congress and later prohibited from wearing it on a CBS broadcast. Designer: Charlie Frick.

East Village Other, cover, July 14, 1971. Fred Mogubgub was an innovative animator who spent many paste-up nights obsessively working on complex, layered fantasies like this one.

New York Review of Sex, cover, February 1969. Copublisher and art director: Steven Heller. Art: "The Blue Sex Goddess of Felix Labisse."

146

CHAPTER 9

I Was a Seventeen-Year-Old Pornographer

hat's how a young assistant prosecuting attorney introduced me to a sleepy Manhattan night court judge as I stood before him in the wee hours of the morning on July 3, 1969. I had been arrested the afternoon before, but because the DA's vice squad detectives didn't know in which downtown Manhattan precinct to book me, we were too late for day court, and so I was held in the adjacent jail known as the tombs until the night session began around 8:00 p.m. Since the docket was full of petty criminals, prostitutes, and drug dealers, I didn't go before the judge until two in the morning. I spent hours being moved from one over-crowded holding cell to another—like passing through the digestive tract of the criminal justice system—until I was finally spit out into a brightly lit courtroom.

I was the art director, designer, and copublisher of the *New York Review of Sex & Politics*, an odd mix of New Left politics, puerile humor, and sexploitation. *NYRS&P* had grown out of the underground newspaper the *New York Free Press* after it was discovered that the *Freep* only sold out when nudes (preferably women) were put on its cover. Like staff at the other New York undergrounds in 1969 (the *East Village Other* and *Rat*), we at the *Free Press* started a sex paper to subsidize our political publication. However, after a month or so of simultaneous publishing, we reluctantly folded the *Freep* and devoted our energies to the sex paper.

I was pasting up our fourth issue when we received a telephone call. "That was the DA's office," said the office manager nervously. "They said that you, Sam, and Jack [the editor and copublisher, respectively] were under arrest and should not leave the premises." Sam Edwards was on an errand, and Jack Banning had absconded with all the money in our bank account a week before and couldn't be located.

I broke into a cold sweat. I was alone and underage. I called our lawyer. He was in a meeting and couldn't be disturbed. "I'm about to be arrested," I told the secretary frantically.

"I'll give him the message," she said calmly.

Next, I called our distributor, a nasty little man whose relatives were related to the infamous Murder, Inc. mobsters during the thirties. His secretary said that he had been called by the DA's office and had left the premises.

Finally, I called my father (I still lived at home). He was out too. For God's sake, where was everyone? I told his secretary to tell him I was being arrested and would probably be home late for dinner.

The moment I hung up the phone, two detectives entered the office. Both looked surprisingly familiar. I had seen the young one on the TV news a few nights before talking about investigating the mob in New York. The heavyset one had come by the office a week before to buy copies of the newspaper. He claimed to be an adult bookseller from Long Island. They showed their badges, read me my rights, and asked the whereabouts of my two partners. I told them I had no idea. I asked if I could go to the bathroom. They came with me while I tied my shoulder-length hair in a ponytail just in case the stories I had heard about goings on in jail were true. I asked if they wanted to handcuff me; they said no, unless I was planning an escape.

As I sat between them in the front seat of their unmarked car, they informed me that all the sex-paper publishers and distributors were being rounded up. "We figured you'd all be at Woodstock," said the heavyset one. He had heard on the radio that the rock festival, which began that day, was attracting thousands of people. "I would like to go," admitted the young one, but he said he had to work. "I decided to work this weekend, too," I volunteered, although I really had planned on going.

(Left) *New York Review of Sex*, cover, June 15, 1969. Copublisher and art director: Steven Heller. Photographer: Mario Jorrin. (Right) *New York Review of Sex*, cover, May 1, 1969. Copublisher and art director: Steven Heller. Photographer: Robert Ferraro.

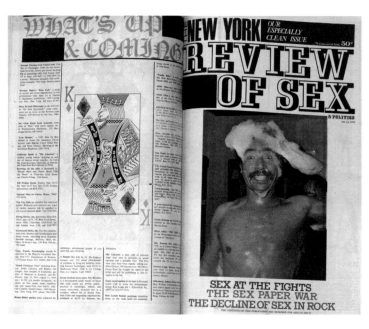

(Top left) *New York Review of Sex*, cover, July 15, 1969: "Our Especially Clean Issue."
This edition was busted for pandering by the Manhattan District Attorney. Photographer:
Mario Jorrin. Illustrator (back page): Roger Tomlinson. (Bottom) Lefthand page:
New York Review of Sex, editorial page. Illustrator: Brad Holland. Righthand page:
Page three was reserved for goofy fetish photos. Copublisher and art director: Steven Heller.

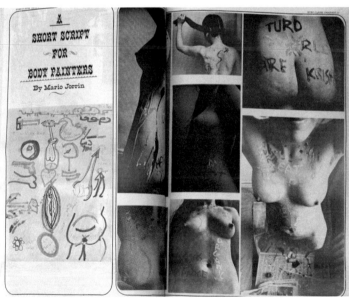

(Top) *New York Review of Sex*, cover, July I, 1969: "Self Gratification" issue.
Photographer: Mario Jorrin. (Bottom) *New York Review of Sex*,
center spread: "A Short Script for Body Painters." Copublisher and art director:
Steven Heller. Photographer: Mario Jorrin.

OUR MAN IN THE BIG APPLE

By D. Melmoth

VOL. I No. 2
APRIL 1, 1969

co-publishers/editors:Jack Banning, Steven Heller, S. Edwards editor:D. Melmoth art director:Steven Heller assistant to the editors: Marianna Milbert movies Gregory Battcock hard news:Peter Johnson, Ray Schultz advertising Sue Ungaro calendar Marianna Milbert

The New York Review of Sex is published bi-weekly by the New York Review of Sex, suite 23, 200 West 72 Street, N.Y.C., 10023. Tel: TR-4-2838

The contents are copyright 1969 by The New York Review of Sex.

The publishers of this newspaper are reluctantly forced to disclaim the first item in our editors column that follows. While not wishing to be in the position of precensoring anything in this paper (obviously contradictory to the spirit of NYRS) we cannot remain silent when innuendo, rumor and unsupported charges, the very sort of hearsay evidence we supposedly stand in opposition to, is published in a prominent place in a publication that bears our names as publishers and editors J.B, S.P.E., S.H.

Usually reliable sources have told us (for a price) that a "big man from Italy" is coming to the Metropolitan area after the convention of organized crime in Miami in order to referee a dispute between New York and New Jersey based mob interests over jurisdiction of a "new property." That new property is reportedly the underground press, or in our informant's words "those properties with the hard sex shuck." They'll have to compete with a lot of other special interest groups who have recently made it their business to influence editorial policy of the old undergrounds, the sexploitation tabloids such as the *ENQUIRER* (put out by the same Pope brothers who sponsor all that Italian heritage and run a straight wire to the tracks), *National Spotlite Midnight*, etc. Along with a little tit display and a lot of random violence, these papers have developed a strong law and order/pro Vietnam editorial policy. An editorial in the March l0 issue of *Midnight* entitled "KILL ALL COMMIE FAMILIES," asks that we "kill your enemy's fighting men! Kill his children! Kill his wounded! Kill his prisoners! Kill his women! Bomb them! Burn them! Stave them! Poison them!..."

In the "new" undergrounds, they'll have to contend with a potpourri of other pressure groups, the Motherfuckers at *RAT*, SDS at whatever will provide free hot lunches, and recently Women's Liberation at *The Great Speckled Bird* (P.O. Box 7946, Station C, Atlanta, Georgia 30309), along with co-option by 'straight' business interests such as the record industry throughout the underground and those behind THIS PUBLICATION (itself which is run straight for profit by the publishers strictly out to make a buck (the first issue's press run of 20,000 copies sold out in less than a week and this issue has a press run of 50,000.)*In fact, this columnist has been under considerable pressure from the publishers not to print this column. They feel that not only is it unethical to blow the whistle on one's compatriots, as well as being bad for business, but who are we to sound so righteous. Well they're right, we're not so righteous, but the point is that the underground makes a fetish of its rightness (and we're interested in other people's fetishes) as opposed to other people's straightness, and devotes without exception some part of each issue of its newspapers to 'structural analysis' of straight institutions to find out who and what the special interests are. Since this newspaper is out to make a buck and is considered revisionist by the underground it's only fair that we give back a little tit for tat.*

Mob infiltrated publishing services in New York (printing and distribution) believe that sex oriented underground press is getting very big all over the country (some 300 odd underground papers) and feel organized crime should get a piece of the action before they are beat out by so called 'hip legitimate business.' (Their interest was first aroused by the success of CAPITOL RECORDS' subsidization of underground papers through advertising contracts.)

This column has been told that eventual mafia control is a real possibility because legitimate printers, distributors, advertisers and investment sources are reluctant to tarnish their reputations by dealing with the papers ("a cunt is a cunt and no big thing but those fucking undergrounds will sneak the American flag in the bush every time") because of local pressure and vague legal protections. Our source concluded "We can do here what we did in the cutlery and garbage industries. Nobody wanted and we got."

MEANWHILE local Jersey officials have been harassing shops that print the undergrounds (all the New York papers print in Jersey because it was cheaper) and mob controlled printers have gone along and made no attempt to 'influence' zealous local officials to keep hands off.

A case in point is that of the *East Village Other*, an underground paper out of New York with about 50,000 circulation. On Tuesday evening, February 18, EVO switched from "Jersey's only straight distributor" to a distributor on Long Island. That same evening EVO also switched printers from a Jersey printer to a printer on Long Island.

Through intermediaries in the printing industry ("Five foot ten and stacked, hanging around the door of EVO in the guise of a groupie–EVO is located in Bill Graham's Fillmore East) it is said that key staff members of EVO have been actively recruited ever since they were taken off the newstands for obscenity some months ago. These members or member were evidently hooked by the evening of the 18th, which was coincidentally the occasion for the convening (of underground press editors at the house of John Wilcock of *Other Scenes* (information gained from said double agent groupie) for discussion of a mutual defense treaty in the face of suppression ("it was decided by all parties present in a consensus vote carried out democratically to picket the Sheridan Square newstand which just won't carry our newspapers from noon Wednesday March 5, just across from the *Village Voice* which won't carry our advertising.")

The EVO delegation reportedly pushed diligently for a common distributor (unnamed) and a common printer..."What the hell, you think the local cops will fuck with Thomas (Tommy Ryan) Eboli and those meat-packing cats?"

ED NOTE: Though left out in original copy it seems to me that it goes without saying that the new "life style" recognizes you get help where you find it and consequently a publication is as independent as it wants to be. For instance, EVO is a better paper now than a year ago.

(continued on p. 15)

New York Review of Sex editorial page, April I, 1969. Copublisher and art director: Steven Heller. Illustrator: Brad Holland.

They asked me exactly what I did. The question seemed innocent enough that to reply without a lawyer being present would not jeopardize my case. "I'm the art director," I said.

"What's that mean? Do you photograph the models?" asked the heavy one.

"No, I design the format, pick the typefaces, crop the pictures, buy the illustrations, paste-up the mechanicals, and sometimes work the typesetting machine, and I get paid very little in the bargain," I said.

During the time it took to find the booking precinct and then get us down to the courthouse for arraignment, the young one and I developed a good rapport. He told me that he really didn't want to arrest me, or any other art director; he was after the mob. He detested the mob and pledged to disrupt as many of its operations as possible. "But we're not mobsters," I said. "Maybe our distributors are, but all newspaper distributors, restaurant suppliers, and private trash disposal companies are mob run. We're just trying to publish an underground paper that takes jabs at authority and hypocrisy." I told them that my Murder, Inc. distributor accused me of being the only person in New York who could make a sex paper fail.

Incidentally, the issue they were busting us on was called "Our Especially Clean Issue." The only vaguely hard-core sex photograph in the issue was an ad for *Screw* (four months earlier, I had been the first art director of *Screw*). Everything else was not only soft-core but no-core; the hottest picture in the issue was a fully clothed woman in a raincoat sitting on a fire hydrant. Nevertheless, some good citizen had complained to the DA's office about the sex papers, and that was impetus enough for the vice squad to take action.

When I reached the jail, a few of my elder colleagues from the other sex papers had already been processed and were ready to make their courtroom appearances. My arresting officers hastily tried to get me through the clogged system, but without success. When the court authorities found out I was still a minor (my eighteenth birthday was only days away), I was put through even more red tape before I was allowed to appear in court. As a minor, I could not be in the male criminal holding cells, so I was placed in a pen with the prostitutes until I was called before the judge. While I scarfed down their bologna sandwiches and Kool-Aid (that day's holding-pen rations), they teased me and played with my ponytail until my name was called. When I entered the courtroom, I found that my distributor had provided a lawyer, and I was released without bail pending trial.

New York Review of Sex and Politics, October 15, 1969. Brad Holland refreshed
the type and used only illustration in the next four issues. Copublisher and
art director: Steven Heller.

New York Review of Sex and Politics, cover, November I, 1969. Our distributor argued that these covers designed and illustrated by Brad Holland would never sell on the newsstand.

155

In the period between my arrest and trial, I was arrested again in another roundup. This time I was eighteen, and the process was not as much fun. My elder partners and I were placed in a huge holding cell full of drunks, vagrants, and petty crooks. My partner Sam, always the comedian, even tried bartering me for a few cigarettes, but mercifully without success.

We learned that these roundups of publishers and distributors were intended to be harassing enough to put us out of business, because the DA really had skimpy legal grounds for censoring our publications. No matter how sexy and sexist they were, the DA could not prove they were pornographic. Indeed, one of the indictments against *Kiss*, the sex paper published by the *East Village Other*, cited an R. Crumb cartoon for obscenity. The cases against all the papers were thrown out of court, but only after a costly legal battle.

After our second arrest, the *New York Review of Sex & Politics* was on its last legs. Our distributor gave us an ultimatum: either we include enough hard-core sex to interest a viable readership or he'd fold us. Our response was to add "& Aerospace" to the already cumbersome title, include even more political content, and ultimately call the publication the *NYRS&P* (*& Aerospace*)—not even mentioning sex in the title. My mentor Brad Holland designed the first new *NYRS&P* cover using an illustration that was so soft-core that the paper looked somewhat like its unprofitable forerunner, the *Free Press*. Brad designed and illustrated two more. I did the final cover, spelling out the title with a cropped art photo of a very beautiful nude Black woman. The distributor cut us off and the paper died.

Nevertheless, I was still under indictment. I still had to appear in court on porn charges. And I still faced a possible prison sentence if convicted. Art direction was a mighty dangerous job.

By this time, we had a reputable First Amendment lawyer, Herald Price Fahringer, who was paid by our former distributor. Herald later went on to defend the tabloid favorites Jean Harris, who killed her lover, and Claus von Bülow, who poisoned his wife. (He lost both murder cases.)

Herald's strategy was to petition a three-judge panel prior to our initial trial on the grounds that the *NYRS&P* and *Screw* were unlawfully censored, citing prior restraint. The judges had to determine whether the DA was indeed harassing us or, based on the content of the paper, had a reasonable cause for confiscating issues and arresting principals. They were

New York Review of Sex and Politics, November 1969. Our distributor claimed:
"I was the only publisher in New York that could make a sex paper fail."
This was the final issue. Photographer unknown.

also to determine whether each issue could be reviewed by judges before warrants were issued, or if that was also unconstitutional. The legalities were complex, but fundamental. Somehow during the blitz of briefs and testimony, it was determined that the DA did not adhere to the law, and we were exonerated on all charges before going to trial. The *NYRS&P* had folded, and I returned, after a year hiatus at *Rock* magazine, to art direction at *Screw*.

Winning this case meant that New York City and New York State legal authorities left the sex papers alone, and *Screw* took every opportunity to see how far that tolerance could be stretched. During my two-year tenure as art director, the legal actions against *Screw* were minor. But shortly after I left my stint, the feds indicted *Screw* in Wichita, Kansas (the hub of the US Postal Service) for pandering through the mail. This was not taken lightly, since Ralph Ginzburg, former publisher of the legendary *Eros*, had been found guilty and imprisoned on similar charges.

Given my experience, I knew that before *Screw* could be convicted for pornography it must be proven that it was void of any redeeming social value, which, without excusing its rampant sexism, it had. It was a journal of cultural criticism pegged to sex. I knew that as art director I could help *Screw* pass muster if ever it was judicially scrutinized by maintaining a high level of design and illustration to offset the truly awful photography. Hence, I suggested that Push Pin Studios (Milton Glaser and Seymour Chwast) redesign *Screw* in 1971, which they did, though badly. Milton designed a clever visual pun for the logo, with the middle stroke of the *E* in *Screw* turned upward like an erect penis; all the other design letters were corporate-looking Helvetica. The interior layouts were lackluster.

I hired some of the best artists—including Brad Holland, Marshall Arisman, Edward Sorel, Mick Haggerty, Philippe Weisbecker, Jan Faust, Don Ivan Punchatz, and John O'Leary—to draw and paint exclusive illustrations for the covers. Doug Taylor even won an American Institute of Graphic Arts award for one of his covers. Many of the covers were witty commentaries on sex and sexual politics. I took a similar approach to inside art too. Whenever I could, I'd replace bad photography with good illustration. Some illustrations, however, did not live up to that standard and were just plain dumb.

My strategy was put to the test when, only a few months after I left *Screw* for the *New York Times*, I was subpoenaed to appear first before a federal grand jury and afterward as a hostile witness for the Wichita federal prosecutor in the trial against *Screw*. Unlike the Warren Commission, these proceedings can now be told. I was warned that if I refused to testify, I would be imprisoned for contempt, yet little did they know I wouldn't miss this for the world.

When it came time for me to testify, the prosecutor (whose wife mysteriously sat behind his desk in the courtroom knitting a scarf like Madame Defarge in *A Tale of Two Cities*) showed me large blowups of some of *Screw*'s more prurient pages taken from two or three issues. He asked me to explain how they were put together, what contribution I made to the makeup, and, most critical to his case, what artistic merit they had. I detailed the way type was set, the distinctions between typefaces, and the decisions that lead to the design. I admitted that some pictures might be distasteful even to me, but that the publication in its entirety had great artistic merit. While reminding the jury I was a hostile witness, the prosecutor tried to prove otherwise.

Under cross examination, Herald also brought forth blowup pages, most from issues that included illustration. He asked what each drawing depicted, who did the drawing, and what was the rationale for using a drawing, not a photograph. Each question was a planned opening to wax poetical about the art, describe the achievements of the artists (that is, Brad Holland appears regularly on the Op-Ed page of the *New York Times*, does covers for *Time* magazine, has been honored by the Society of Illustrators and the Art Directors Club, teaches at Pratt Institute, etcetera). With each description of a distinguished artist, the case for redeemability was reinforced and the prosecutor's case faded away.

After a brief deliberation, the jury brought in a verdict of not guilty. Herald said that calling me as prosecution witness was a major mistake for the feds, because my testimony solidly helped convince the jury to accept the defense of social redeemability. This was the last time I was involved with pornography.

On the phone from my office on West 14th Street, telling our mob-connected
printer, Sal, that his print job of *Mobster Times* was unacceptable.

CHAPTER 10

The Mob Boss

A drive through the New Jersey wetlands can be quite enjoyable, but not when the invitation comes in the form of a threat from Sal, a hulk of a guy with reputed ties to the underworld. He ran a printing firm, and I was upset with the quality of a very special new publication, *Mobster Times*, that we, the staff of *Screw*, had hoped would give us entrée to the mass magazine market. But the printing had not gone as I planned, so I hired some people to go to a bindery in Jersey and tear up ten thousand magazine covers that Sal's printing company had screwed up.

"Stevie, Stevie," he said over the phone in a heavy New York basso, "you can't do this, babe. You're costing me money."

"I'm sorry, Sal," I said with a quiver, but firmly holding my ground. "The job stinks, and I just can't let it go through."

After a brief silence, Sal muttered, "Okay, let's take a ride to the bindery. I'll pick you up."

Fifteen minutes later, he pulled up in front of my office in his block-long white Caddy convertible. I got in. He looked over and smiled in a menacing manner. What was I doing, going alone with Sal to Jersey? I asked myself.

"Don't worry, Stevie," he replied, as if reading my mind. "We'll settle this shit once and for all." And so began what I thought was the last car ride of my life.

You see, it was 1972, and I was the art director and cofounder of *Mobster Times*, a magazine started by the publishers of *Screw*, for which I was also art director, which commented on the political scandals that were beginning to brew during the Nixon administration. The publication was also a blatantly vindictive response to *Screw*'s former art directors, Larry Brill and Les Waldstein, who had fallen into disfavor when they'd left the *Screw* family and started their own magazine called *Monster Times*. Nevertheless, our magazine was a serious effort to make a topical humor magazine that reported on new trends in white-collar crimes while appealing to an audience that savored true-crime stories. It was also *Screw*'s first foray into non-sex publishing. In fact, the first issue—which had the title "Crime Does Pay" and whose editorial page showed photographs of *Screw*'s publishers and me in faux Al Capone fedoras, mockingly pointing real guns at the reader—was edited by a respected pseudonymous author of crime books.

This first issue included an interview with the journalist Gay Talese, who had just finished researching the life of mob kingpin Joseph Bonanno (his book was later made into a television movie); a story by Noel Hynd on fake nuns who begged for money in the subways; a visual feature on Richard Nixon's brother's shady dealings with Howard Hughes; and a quiz to determine the world's greatest mobster (the answer was FBI Director J. Edgar Hoover). But the *"tour de farce"* was a review of the newly released film *The Godfather*, purportedly written by the soon-to-be-slain goodfella Joseph (Joey) Gallo, as told to publisher Al Goldstein. Our first cover, which I made myself, featured a sepia photograph of Al Capone (our mascot) shot with bullet holes.

Since *Screw*'s publishers believed that *Mobster Times* was as potentially viable as the *National Lampoon* (which in 1973 was in its heyday), they wanted to avoid the *Screw* distribution apparatus of mob delivery men and instead find a national distributor. They approached a few, but only Curtis—the venerable and conservative publisher of the *Saturday Evening Post*, *Holiday*, and scores of other household magazines—was the least bit interested. Actually, Curtis had overdiversified, had fallen on hard times, and was looking for an easy income vehicle.

The *Mobster Times* crew: me, Al Goldstein, and Jim Buckley.
Photographer: Eric Stephen Jacobs.

Since we were producing the magazine entirely on our own, Curtis put up a very small cash investment and agreed to take us on. But even with the promise of national distribution, we could not afford full-color printing on slick paper, so *Mobster Times*'s interior was printed on newsprint by *Screw*'s cheapo web press printer (also run by guys with mob connections). The least we wanted, however, was for the cover to be printed on glossy stock at Sal's shop. Herein the trouble began.

Sal, you see, printed sexually hard-core adult material for which quality control was not a major concern. He didn't always print this kind of XXX-rated stuff, nor was he always wealthy—driving luxury cars and all. In fact, he used to work on small, run-of-the-mill jobs and was a perfect candidate for debtor's prison when allegedly his business was "acquired" by—well, you get the picture—who proceeded to keep the half dozen multiliths working throughout the nights and on weekends printing a genre of smut called T&A (tits and ass) books. While I have no idea how the business worked, the T&A was distributed by the new owners, who distributed other sensitive material

Mobster Times cover, August 1972. Upon deciding to publish a magazine on crime,
I developed three signature tropes: the black hand as a trademark, the *o* in the masthead as
a gunsight, and Al Capone as the mascot. I designed and art directed all three issues.

as well. What I can report is that whenever a grand jury was impaneled to investigate strong-arm tactics and takeovers in the publishing and printing industries, Sal would turn on his answering machine and take an extended vacation to some tropical paradise. What a tan he had too.

When Sal's silent partner and business associate, whom I called Mr. DB, learned that *Screw* was publishing another magazine that was destined to be distributed by someone else, he called for an immediate lunch meeting at Umbertos Clam House—the legendary goodfella meeting place. This was the very same Umbertos where, a few weeks later, notorious capo Joseph Gallo was summarily gunned down in a hail of bullets, initiating a yearlong gangland conflict— the kind of scenario that films are made of. The conversation was as heavy as the Chicken Parmesan. It began with Mr. DB's threatening inquiry, "So what the fuck is this new venture you got going?"

Before lunch, Al and I had worried that Mr. DB would be disturbed by the content of *Mobster Times*— with emphasis on the word *mobster*. We thought he might take personal offence. Instead, he was annoyed by the political content. He

Mobster Times advertising sticker, 1972.
I wrote most of the advertising copy and slogans.
Art director: Steven Heller.

stared at me as the weakest link: "Well, sir, it's a magazine about Nixon and political corruption," I offered. "We didn't think you'd be interested in it…"

"I'm interested in everything that's sold on the newsstand," Mr. DB corrected me, "especially when it's produced by someone with whom I have a relationship. With you I have a relationship! You sure this isn't another sex paper?"

THE SUPPRESSED DISNEYWORLD PAPERS 💦💦 FAKE NUNS EXPOSED
💦 GAY TALESE INSIDE THE MAFIA 💦 AN INDUSTRIAL SPY TELLS ALL 💦

DELL-04399

MOBSTER TIMES

75¢   OCTOBER/No. 2

RETAILERS: SEE RETAIL DISPLAY AGREEMENT, PAGE 50.

Mobster Times, cover, October 1972. It was Brad Holland's idea to repaint
Rembrandt van Rijn's *The Wardens of the Amsterdam Drapers' Guild* with a lineup
of sundry criminal portraits. Art director: Steven Heller.

Mobster Times, cover, December 1972. This issue (number three) was the final one. While we were planning an issue number four, sales were sagging and the plug was pulled. Art director: Steven Heller. Illustrator: Tom Hachtman.

167

BE THE
FIRST ON YOUR BLOCK.

SUBSCRIBE TO MOBSTER TIMES.

MOBSTER TIMES comes out every other month. But what if your local newsstand or prison canteen doesn't carry it? What if your FBI agent who's got you pegged for the gangster you are? What if your fingernails are tapped? What if there's a black limo waiting near your favorite cigar store with five angry mobsters on the lookout for you with a contract in their hands and sights on their guns? Why wait in line anyway, with the rest of the crowd pushing and shoving trying to plunk down your hard-earned payola for the latest issue? With a little forethought you can pass the wee hours with your own 'MOBSTER TIMES without ever stepping out at all! "How," you ask? How can you sneak your MOBSTER TIMES past the guards and the rest of the boys? By subscribing, that's how. Every issue of MOBSTER TIMES will come in a special envelope, addressed personally to you with the familiar seal of the black hand plastered over the front of it. And receipt is guaranteed by the crooks in the United States Postal Service, who are forced, under the strictest regulations, to hand it over to you. It might pass a few grubby postal fists along its way to you, but—you'll get it! So whether you're a warden or a convict, a winner or a loser, a cop or a gangster, or simply a person of high standing in your community, a subscription to MOBSTER TIMES is the answer to all those unanswered questions, whatever they may be. Like, "How the hell do I get out of here?" or "How many days have I got left?" or "What's the best way to quell a prison riot?"

In the next issue of MOBSTER TIMES you'll be amazed while reading the interview with Gay Talese, author of **Honor Thy Father**, the story of Bill Bonnano and his "family" background; "The Disneyworld Papers," the incredible story behind the Northern Florida coup d'etat led by the forces of evil in the person of Walt Disney; "The Bogus Nuns," the true tale of how you, or anyone, can make a living out of religion—by starting your own!; "How to Run Away From Home," a manual for persons who want to get away from it all—permanently! Next month's "Miss Underworld" will be none other than Xaviera Hollander, the Knapp Commission's surprise prostitute witness. Let her tell you how she helped clean up New York, by cleaning up in New York! Then we'll have "Honest Schmuck of the Month," "This Day in Crime"—an up-to-the-minute Crime Calendar which highlights famous moments in crime from pre-history to the present. And much more, like book reviews, movie reviews, advice columns from "Changing Your Identity" to "Avoid Being Spotted." Look for it all in the MOBSTER TIMES you'll get on your newsstand or at your door. The choice is yours.

P.S. Take a tip from Jim the Blade, a gift subscription to MOBSTER TIMES is just what the doctor ordered for your "penpal" inside. There's no better way to his heart or cell than tips, stories and gags from his buddies on the outside!

You can begin a steady diet of MOBSTER TIMES by sending $6.00 for the next 12 issues to: MOBSTER TIMES, P.O. Box 431, Old Chelsea Station, New York City, N.Y. 10011. Make it payable to: MOBSTER TIMES. Then stick it in an envelope with your name and address (be sure to include your zip—no, not your zip gun, your zip **code**). Put a stamp on it and "drop it" at the most convenient mailbox in sight. Then run back home quickly. Or buy it on your local newsstand. Bu whatever you do, buy it. Or else.*

*This is not a reminder, this is a threat.

One of my favorite subscription ads, from 1972; I've always loved visual and verbal puns. Art director: Steven Heller.

MOBSTER TIMES

crime does pay

The Blade

The Punk

Big Al

THE GANG

Publisher
Friday 13th Publishing Co.
Editor
Jim "The Blade" Buckley
Executive Editor
"Big" Al Goldstein
Art Director
Steve "Punk Kid" Heller
Managing Editor
Paul "The Heater" Raley
Asst. Art Directors
Howard Karsh, Ruth Ross
Advertising Manager
Marcia "Moose" Blackman
Production
Peter Ogren

MOBSTER TIMES is published by Friday 13th Publishing Co., 116 West 14th St., New York City 10011. Tel: (212) 989-1660. Office hours: Mon.-Fri. —10a.m. to 6p.m.

WHAT'S IT ALL ABOUT

MOBSTER TIMES will set out to undo the twisted set of values that glorify crooks on the one hand and slap their wrists with the other. When kids play cops and robbers, very few of them want to be the cops. Only the finks choose to be Eliot Ness, whereas everybody wants to be "Bugsy" Moran or "Big" Al Capone. What happened? Where did we go wrong? We've been brainwashed, that's what. We've been led to believe that all cops, DAs and G-men are goody-goodys whose sole ambition in life is to shoot gangsters, while the gangster is always surrounded with all the good things life has to offer—booze, plenty of free cash, beautiful women—and when he dies, he dies heroically. The cop always lives in a semi-slum tenement, has an ugly or not so attractive wife and a couple of brats to worry about not feeding some night. The gangster lives in a fancy apartment, has no responsibility except to himself and just has to make sure of his place in the big "family." This kind of twisted attitude was bound to screw up some of our misplaced youth. But MOBSTER TIMES will change all that! MOBSTER TIMES will readjust the old-time formula—kids will want to play cop again when they realize how much brighter and more successful cops have been in nailing down big profits—and with fewer risks!

That's right, MOBSTER TIMES will deal with real life. There are a lot of cops on the take who live high and kick their heels (see the Knapp Commission on New York City Police Corruption for more details), there are District Attorneys who make a living out of headlines (Thomas E. Dewey , for instance, who hounded Lucky Luciano into jail, then freed him a decade later on the verge of becoming President of the U.S.). All the spoils don't go to the gangster—and to dispel this warped vision of United States history and return this nation's youth on the right path, MOBSTER TIMES is here.

FOR INSTANCE

Who gained more out of his madness, Lyndon B. Johnson or George Metesky, the infamous "Mad Bomber" of New York? Who did more for the working man, Henry Ford or James Hoffa? It's hard to figure who was the bigger crook, but we all know who spent more time in the can. Billy Sol Estes spent less than two years in prison for robbing the government and the public out of millions of dollars, but people regularly spend 5 years and more for small-time robberies. Who would YOU rather be?

Out of this mish-mash of justice and crime MOBSTER TIMES has devised an ingenious formula to ascertain a criminal's worth: Crime + Magnitude = Respect. In other words, if George Metesky had improved his technique, he too could have a $40 million edifice glorifying his life like the LBJ Library in Houston, Texas, but instead he was relegated to history's footnotes through incompetence and a general ignorance of the proper know-how to become a big-time mobster. If he had read MOBSTER TIMES, he'd have known how to make the most out of a couple of smart lawyers and sympathetic judges. Remember, a grand in time saves nine.

WHAT ARE OUR PLANS?

MOBSTER TIMES plans to keep you informed: how to tell if your phone is being tapped, how to tap other people's phones. How to spot a Federal Agent, how to BECOME a Fed, how to take over a country—and where those countries are. How to move in on UNsuccessful businesses and make the most of them, how to move in on SUCCESSFUL businesses and make the most of them, too. How to talk right—one of the most important requisites for a successful criminal is that he speak the part. In other words—if you talk like a small-time hood, you'll be treated like one—and if you carry yourself with style and wit, you'll become the hit of the jury and the darling of the front page. So, let's work together to get America on its feet again. Let's sing the praises of the men and women who made this country great. Let's put John D. Rockefeller, Joe Kennedy, Al Capone, Meyer Lansky, Lyndon Johnson, Aaron Burr back on the right side of the fence. Let's educate the masses so that your kids and theirs will want to play J. Edgar Hoover as well as Dutch Schultz, and get America going again. Just you and me and MOBSTER TIMES! —Jim Buckley

The masthead and first editorial for *Mobster Times*, August 1972.

Opening page for two-part interview with Gay Talese in *Mobster Times*. Talese had just finished writing a book on mob boss Joe Bonanno. Designer: Steven Heller.

Opening page of the "Disneyworld Papers" exposé in *Mobster Times*, August 1972. To this day, I'm not certain whether this story on the CIA's involvement with Disney was fact or fiction. Designer: Steven Heller.

GREAT MOMENTS IN CRIME No. 1

Al Capone gets Syphilis

Brought to you by COOTCHIE HOOTCH® "THE BREW THAT SLAPS YOU ON THE
BACK WITH ONE HAND & PICKS YOUR POCKET WITH THE OTHER."
Next month's GREAT MOMENT IN CRIME: John Dillinger shops for prophylactics

© 1972 BY UNEEDA BREWERIES OF CHICAGO, MILWAUKEE & TENAFLY, N.J.

"Great Moments in Crime" was a regular *Mobster Times* feature conceived by
Brad Holland to showcase political issues, August 1972. Our mascot died of syphilis while
serving his sentence. Illustrator: Brad Holland. Art director: Steven Heller.

GREAT MO— —CRIME No.3

By Brad Holland

Birth of the Nixonburger

Howard Hughes, the well-renowned but seldom encountered moneybags, chomps into a $135,000 Nixon-
burger at famous NIXON'S restaurant in L.A. The wacky millionaire, who prefers not to mix it up with the
hoi polloi, made a pre-dawn visit to the burger emporium lorded over by Nixon's colorless brother, Donald.
But Hughes shut up tight as a virgin when asked why he was willing to pay such a pretty penny for a burger
with fries.

Next Month's Great Moment in Crime: John Dillinger shops for prophylactics.

© 1972 by Nixon's Restaurant, a partially owned subsidiary of Hughes Tool & Die Company (TOOLCO) & Hughes
Political Philanthropies (SLUSH).

PRINTED IN U.S.A.

This October 1972 "Great Moments in Crime" commented on
the questionable business relationship between Howard Hughes and
President Richard Nixon's brother Donald. Art director: Steven Heller.

173

The Death of Dutch Schultz · By Ray Schultz

DEWEY UNTO OTHERS BEFORE THEY DEWEY UNTO YOU!

Opening page for a story in *Mobster Times* on the mobster Dutch Schultz
by our reporter Ray Schultz (no relation), August 1972. Art director: Steven Heller.

(Left) Parody cover for *Mobster Times*, December, 1972. Special feature
titled the "Misfortune Society Newsletter" featuring a comic story about celebrity
death row convict Caryl Chessman, who became a jailhouse author of four books.
(Right) Opening page for a story on famous New York madame Polly Adler by
Lynda Crawford, August 1972. Art director: Steven Heller.

175

I shook my head from side to side. "Definitely no sex at all," I said impetuously, looking at Al to jump in with his rapier wit. After all, I was only twenty-two, and, since I did not have the good sense to get a respectable job, here I was at lunch with Mr. DB, a high-ranking capo, just a heartbeat away from making a jerk of myself. "This is about crime in high places," I rambled on, "like J. Edgar Hoover, who has abused his power for decades, and Richard Nixon, who's doing God knows what to screw our system, or..."

"Okay, okay, I get the picture," Mr. DB interrupted, noticeably impatient. "So, this is another one of those crackpot, commie, hippie underground papers, right? That's what is sounds like. And you're right—I don't want anything to do with it!"

"Unless it turns a profit!?" quipped Sal.

"Yeah right," Mr. DB replied, making it clear he had voted for Nixon.

"But what about the printing?" Al pressed, "We print with you, right?"

"Well, only as a favor to you, Al," Mr. DB said, a little less annoyed and decidedly deferential. "But I don't even want to see any of that commie crap. Are we clear!?"

If *Mobster Times* had been devoted to the heroes of the underworld, would Mr. DB have been a tad more enthusiastic? Regardless, he allowed us to print on his presses, saving us plenty of dough.

Yet we still weren't out of the woods.

After putting the content and design together, we decided to take out ads in the *New York Times*, *Daily News*, and *Village Voice*. We printed up posters and stickers using our mascot pic of Capone with my headline: "Now there's a magazine for him, *Mobster Times*." I designed a typographically elegant display ad that explained what we wanted to accomplish. The newspaper ads were timed to coincide with the massive (for us) publicity campaign that included a press conference, press release, and publicity package that would include promo copies. We pumped a lot of loot into the promotion, and we'd only break even if we sold more than one thousand subscriptions. Since Curtis didn't offer a penny to help, we could lose a lot of money. Everyone was poised for the launch.

I went out to the bindery to supervise the first edition. After a few hours of watching the interior being printed, my eyes were drawn to the corner of the plant and a pallet full of our color covers. It wasn't what I had expected. Mr. DB wasn't kidding; it looked like they had been printed late at night and probably by a sight-impaired pressman. I sensed that something was amiss, so I cut the plastic ties to find that every other cover was washed out—the black border surrounding the Capone photograph was gray and the sepia was dull red. In a fit of pique, I called Sal, trying to reach him on his new car phone. He didn't answer. Then I called Al. He told me, "Don't wait for Sal, just destroy them."

"How?"

"Hire some guys."

"Where do I get these guys?"

The next day a truck load of "friends" were on the loading dock at the bindery tearing covers into thousands of pieces. The binder called Sal. Sal called me. And within an hour or two I was sitting on the white leather seats of Sal's Caddy, listening to Frank Sinatra on 8-track tape, on my way through the Jersey wetlands, possibly to a watery grave. For all I knew he had driven other smart-assed art directors to the same resting place.

Instead, when we arrived at the bindery, Sal looked at the mess and said, "Stevie, you're right, babe, it's my fault. I had a moron working that shift. I'm sorry. We'll reprint, and I'll eat the cost. Just remember what I'm doin' here. I don't want Mr. DB to know."

Whether Mr. DB found out, I'll never know. I never saw Sal again.

CHAPTER 11

My Other Mentor

A rt directors are lightning rods rather than lightning. Few are agents of change. Dugald Stermer, on the other hand, was a force to be reckoned with. For me as a teenager—reading and especially looking at his beloved left-wing magazine *Ramparts*, a tiny island off the coast of the mainstream media—his art direction hit me like gale force winds. Although I was barely old enough to know what art direction was, I found Dugald's name on *Ramparts*'s masthead, and he became one of my leading role models. I knew absolutely nothing about him, but he was doing something with this magazine that churned up my sense of devotion and belonging to a cause.

Ramparts was the clarion of new politics and social mores on the West Coast. It exposed CIA involvement in American colleges and universities and raked up muck by providing an alternative to the dominant American journalism. *Ramparts* nurtured the New Left's emerging energy to fight against the Vietnam War, which, for better or worse, helped foment the revolutionary spirit of the time.

Ramparts was not on the cutting edge of design in the way that, say, *Emigre* was in the 1980s and '90s. Rather, its bookish, nineteenth-century

Ramparts, cover, December 1967. This shows the ritual burning of the magazine staff's personal draft cards. The hand second from right belongs to art director Dugald Stermer. Photographer: Carl Fischer.

Ramparts, cover, January 1967. Dugald's art direction gave the magazine
its heart and soul, and a healthy dose of wit. Photographer: Carl Fischer.

typographic conceits, which ultimately came to define Dugald's design personality, conformed to classical design verities, the most important of which was legibility. This was a magazine to read. Dugald, *Ramparts*'s art director from 1964 to 1970, explained to me that the magazine's restrained format was in deliberate contrast to the underground press's anarchic approach. It "lent credibility to what must have seemed then like hysterical paranoid ravings of loonies," he said.

One of *Ramparts*'s most controversial stories was the confession of a Green Beret sergeant who quit his elite fighting force in protest of the secret war in Vietnam and Cambodia. *Ramparts* drew material from other disaffected government and military personnel whose consciences had been bothering them, but who at that time couldn't air their grievances in major newspapers. For me *Ramparts* was "the word" handed down from San Francisco New Lefties to acolytes throughout the nation.

The mainstream press, including the *New York Times*, was skeptical of anti-government attacks and more or less followed an "America, love it or leave it" stance. Dugald told me that *Ramparts*'s goal was to "just raise hell," although it insisted on journalistic reliability.

Ramparts was not a blind follower of dogma or a passive agent of ideology. Nor was Dugald one to be seduced or corrupted in any way. That was an important lesson. He told me, "We never took anything, not even our own side, at face value. We were skeptical of the hippies and diggers but did not go out of our way to criticize them either, since they weren't the enemy."

Dugald passed on to me, in addition to his pragmatic yet moral standards, his method of art directing of illustration. He was as an illustrator, and he knew how to entice exceptional work from top artists despite the magazine's pauper-like fees. He lured Edward Sorel to *Ramparts* by offering him a monthly visual column, Sorel's Bestiary, where he satirically portrayed famous people as animals. He commissioned many members of Push Pin Studios, including founders Seymour Chwast and Milton Glaser, though they risked undermining their business relationships with their mass-market clients through associating with a left-leaning journal. Robert Grossman did one of his best LBJ caricatures for *Ramparts*, and Paul Davis executed a number of its covers, including one of South Vietnam's First Lady (technically, the president's sister-in-law) Madame Nhu, as a cheerleader for an investigative report into CIA recruitment of operatives for clandestine work in Vietnam.

Ramparts, cover, May 1967. Dugald was extremely proud when he convinced Norman Rockwell to make a portrait of Lord Bertrand Russell.

Dugald proudly bragged to me about his two happiest coups. The first was hiring Ben Shahn out of veritable retirement to do a portrait of the early antiwar senator J. William Fulbright. The second was commissioning Norman Rockwell to paint a portrait of Bertrand Russell. "I thought it would be terrific to have one great man in his seventies paint another in his nineties," he said. Although Rockwell balked at first, apparently his son Tom convinced him that *Ramparts* was more important than the *Saturday Evening Post*.

Dugald's validation for me as an art director was one of the most significant accolades I could earn. I routinely put Dugald on the mailing lists of various underground newspapers, including *Screw*, that I art directed. I

Ramparts, cover, March 1967. Portrait of Stanley Mouse,
half of the poster duo Mouse & Kelley. Photographer: Bob Seidemann.

thought that he would either be disgusted by them and write me a note to cease and desist, or he might be impressed, and even say so. At worst, he could ignore my mailings entirely. Unfathomable as the second option was to me, that's exactly what happened. The first letter he wrote to me produced great joy—one of those high points in life you hear about but rarely experience. Dugald's acknowledgment of the value of my work gave me the wherewithal to continue doing it.

I don't remember how or when we met face to face or how we became close friends, or "pards," as he'd like to say. I called him Duke (which I often pronounced as Duck), and he called me Buck. I'd often get confused and call *him* Buck, but he was tolerant.

Duke became a moral compass—a term I hate, but it is entirely apt here. He instilled in me the truth that the work of designers and illustrators can have consequences.

We once appeared together on stage at some conference in California; the idea was to preach to the assembled multitudes on the evils of doing cigarette packaging or other questionable advertising. It was pretty lame. We both knew it was presumptuous of us to wag our finger, so we arranged to have two stools and two guitars on stage as we spoke. Dugald was a picker, so it made some sense, but I can't play a lick. No matter. We walked on the stage and just sat down on the stools with our instruments, like Greenwich Village folkies, and started to, well, pontificate. Never once did we play a note. It was just one of many idiotic seemed-great-at-the-time ideas I've had, only this time I also convinced Dugald to do it, despite his better judgment. The audience was perplexed. I thought it was hysterical, while Dugald thought I was deluded. But, being a mensch, he joined me in my prank.

The pleasure of knowing Dugald—just knowing he was around, even if we had not talked for months—was very special. He died in 2011. I didn't know he was as ill as he was with a rare skin cancer. I wrote his obituary for the *New York Times*. It was among the saddest and most personal I ever pitched, and I had to write dispassionately, to boot (he'd have loved that I wrote "to boot," because he loved his boots). He left behind legions of people who learned from—and terribly miss—him, from the ex-cons that he weekly counseled at a halfway house in San Francisco to the illustrators he taught daily. There are still times now that I'll dial the phone before I remember he is no longer here. If only post-funerary-transcendental Zoom meeting was possible (it's bound to be developed). Dugald was my BFWC: Best Friend West Coast.

Ramparts, cover, October 1967. A film still of John Lennon in a scene from Richard Lester's satiric film *How I Won The War*, starring Lennon. Art director: Dugald Stermer.

CHAPTER 12

An Evergreen
Memory

Working with (and no less becoming an intimate of) Dugald
Stermer at *Ramparts* was high on my list of aspirations. So was
getting my work in *Evergreen Review*, *Ramparts*'s East Coast equivalent, which published such illustration luminaries as Robert
Grossman, Tomi Ungerer, Edward Sorel, and my mentor Brad Holland,
among other acerbic political satirists. I still have many 1960s issues of
Evergreen that filled my head from empty to full of left-wing ideas.

One of the first art directors at *Evergreen Review* was Roy Kuhlman,
who also designed exquisite covers for *Evergreen*'s publisher, Grove Press.
Another art director was Dick Hess; when I was fifteen, I left him my portfolio for review, came back the next day, and found that it hadn't been
touched. That threw me into a tailspin for a year.

When I was sixteen, I worked up the courage to approach *Evergreen*
again. By then, there was a new art director, Ken Deardorf, who also
designed jazz record album covers. I showed him my skimpy portfolio
filled with unpublished and unpublishable drawings. He kindly
photographed five of them for a card file he kept of all the illustrators
and cartoonists who visited him at the office on University Place and 11th

Closeup: Last Tango In Paris, paperback cover, 1973. Grove Press hired me to design an anthology devoted to criticism of this controversial Bernardo Bertolucci film.

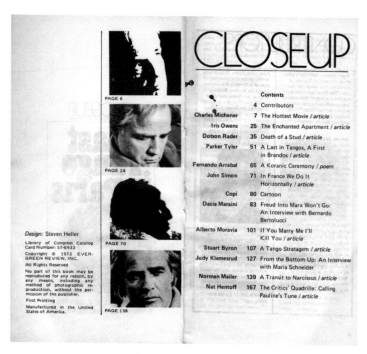

PAGE 6

PAGE 24

PAGE 70

PAGE 138

Design: Steven Heller

Although this is a paperback book, I used a magazine approach of excerpting photographs for *Closeup*'s table of contents. Designer: Steven Heller.

Street. I was so thrilled that he took the time and effort to make me feel professional.

It was a happy surprise for me that around two years later, after no additional communications, I received a call from him suggesting that I take over the art direction job. I couldn't believe that he remembered me, but apparently he'd quietly followed my work. *Evergreen Review* had fallen on hard times, but it continued to occasionally publish as a small paperback book.

I accepted. *Evergreen* had been such a powerful force in my life in newspapers and magazines, and I had high regard for its publisher/editor, Barney Rosset, who was a First Amendment legend.

I met with Rosset a few times during my tenure, which was like touching greatness. He was known as a courageous person who helped change the course of publishing in the United States, bringing masters like Samuel Beckett to Americans' attention under the Grove Press and

THE HOTTEST MOVIE
by Charles Michener

Long before it had its U.S. premiere in New York, Bernardo Bertolucci's *Last Tango in Paris* had kicked up more dust than any movie since Howard Hughes's *The Outlaw* rode into town more than a quarter-century ago and set off a storm of controversy and litigation with its attempt to expose Jane Russell's cleavage. Starring Marlon Brando as a sex-driven, middle-aged dropout, *Tango* was already a *succès de scandale* in France, breaking box office records in Paris, where it opened before Christmas, and provoking a public debate that reduced intellectuals to hysterics. In Italy, authorities confiscated the film, but recently a court in Bologna cleared the movie of charges that it took "persistent delight in arousing base, libidinous instincts." In New York, the distributor, United Artists, carefully decided to open the X-rated film at a small East Side theater on a $5-a-head, reserved-seat basis, to be followed by similar "hard ticket"

7

All the display type was set on a PhotoTypositor using Kabel Light. I made the high-contrast images on a Stat King. Designer: Steven Heller

Black Cat imprints and, as the *New York Times* put it, "winning celebrated First Amendment slugfests against censorship."

During the most memorable meeting we had together, he announced matter-of-factly that for a book about the film *Last Tango in Paris* he had lost all the mechanicals. They were probably thrown out of his hotel room by the cleaning person. Luckily, I had made photostats of all the layouts. We printed from those (needless to say, the quality of typography was horrid).

That late-sixties era was heavy with controversial publishers, known for challenging government's abrogation of the First Amendment, and I worked for many of them. In addition to Barney Rosset and Al Goldstein, there was Maurice Girodias, founder of the Olympia Press in Paris and publisher of Henry Miller, Samuel Beckett, Vladimir Nabokov, and William S. Burroughs. Maurice also published a translation of the contraband *Story of O*. I was asked to design a dummy for a magazine to be called *O*; I did the letterhead, that's all.

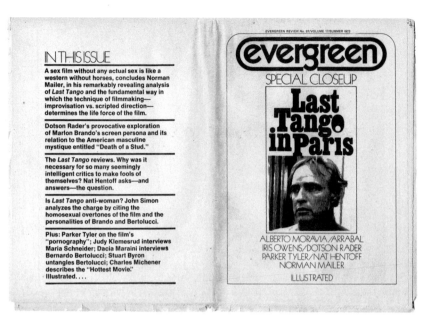

EVERGREEN REVIEW No. 97/VOLUME 17/SUMMER 1973

evergreen

SPECIAL CLOSEUP

Last Tango in Paris

ALBERTO MORAVIA/ARRABAL
IRIS OWENS/DOTSON RADER
PARKER TYLER/NAT HENTOFF
NORMAN MAILER

ILLUSTRATED

A special black-and-white newsprint edition of *Evergreen* was published simultaneously with the book, using the same content, 1973. I never understood the point of having two different formats. Designer: Steven Heller.

Then there was Lyle Stuart, who started as business manager for EC Comics, publisher of *Mad*, and founded Lyle Stuart, Inc. in 1955 with the proceeds of a libel settlement with gossip columnist Walter Winchell. The publishing house was known for *Naked Came the Stranger*, *The Anarchist Cookbook*, and *The Sensuous Woman*. Lyle was a good friend of my boss Al Goldstein, and I was loaned out to work on assorted projects for him.

Back to my work for Grove. I also designed books on Irish liberation and the script for *American Graffiti*, my favorite film. I had seen it before leaving on my first trip to Los Angeles, where my girlfriend and I got into a late-night accident on the Ventura Freeway. My oldest friend, Leigh Hart, owned a 1957 turquoise-and-white finned Chrysler with a push-button transmission, and took us to find a doctor to dress our bruises. He drove the car down the Sunset Strip—just like in *American Graffiti*. When I got back to New York my girlfriend and I had broken up, but a call waited for me asking if I'd like to design the screenplay book. I guess I was fated to win some and lose some.

evergreen
SPECIAL CLOSEUP

Library of Congress Catalog Card Number: 57-6933. EVERGREEN REVIEW is published quarterly by Evergreen Review, Inc., 53 East 11th Street, New York, N.Y. 10003, Barney Rosset, president and treasurer. SUBSCRIPTION RATES: $1.50 per copy; $5.00 four issues; $9.00 eight issues. Foreign postage, including Canada, $1.40 per year additional. Manuscripts will not be returned unless accompanied by stamped, self-addressed envelopes and no responsibility can be assumed for unsolicited material. Copyright © 1973 by EVERGREEN REVIEW, INC. Second Class Postage Paid at New York, N.Y. 10003 and at additional offices. Manufactured in the United States of America.

For the newsprint quarter-folded version of *Evergreen,* I used my favorite table of contents format of cropped images, all reproduced in high contrast.

Interview: Andy Warhol's Film Magazine, cover, July 1971. This issue was devoted to Luchino Visconti's film *Death in Venice.* Art director: Glenn O'Brien. Designer: Steven Heller.

CHAPTER 13

A Warhol Minute

I played a minor role in the history of Andy Warhol's *Interview* magazine, and this is as good a time and place as any to toot my horn. In three or four issues published in 1971, my name appears on *Interview's* masthead under "layout"—not "design" or "designer," but "layout." That year, however, I redesigned *Interview* magazine at the request of Bob Colacello and Glenn O'Brien (who were the editors and ersatz "art director," respectively, and watched over me like hawks). If I do say so, my version was typographically cleaner than that of the handful of previous issues.

When it premiered in 1969 at the Warhol Factory above Union Square in Manhattan (the Factory was just a few blocks away, across Union Square from the legendary nightclub Max's Kansas City), *Interview* was Andy's very own do-it-yourself film magazine, before the term "DIY" became fashionable. It was his toy, but, to be honest, he didn't really design or edit it himself—he had members of his entourage do it for him. In fact, I never met him while working for *Interview*, but his spirit was pervasive, like a bewigged phantom peering through the clouds.

The first half dozen or so issues of *Interview* adhered to the slapdash tradition of late-sixties underground newspapers such as the *East Village*

Other and *Berkeley Barb*. I suppose the design could have been influenced by George Maciunas's Fluxus periodicals, although I never heard any of the *Interview* editors mention Fluxus by name. However, I did see them reading the so-called cheap-chic newsprint fashion magazine *Rags* (published by *Rolling Stone*'s Straight Arrow Publishing Company and where artist Barbara Kruger was a designer in her early years), which was somewhere between under- and middle-ground. John Wilcox's *Other Scenes*, a scrappy

Interview: Andy Warhol's Film Magazine, cover, June 1971. Art director: Glenn O'Brien. Designer: Steven Heller.

underground tabloid edited by one of the founders of the *Village Voice*, was also on the table. Hence *Interview*'s early issues did not exhibit any exceptional design approaches.

As far as I could tell, Andy never got his hands dirty with this rag. He was many blocks from where I was, yet was listed as second on *Interview*'s masthead, under co-editor and *Chelsea Girls* co-director Paul Morrissey. Not only did I never meet with Andy, but also I was never told that he (or Paul) passed on my redesign before it went to press. I still wonder whether they even read the publication.

Simultaneously with my gig at *Interview*, I was art director and designer of *Rock*, a second-tier music tabloid. To make ends meet, *Rock*'s publisher rented typesetting services to *Interview* and other publications. He threw my "talents" in at *Interview* as what in the retail business is called a loss leader—something free to lure customers into the store).

I deserved a more substantive title than "layout" because all the type and graphic choices for the redesign were mine. Instead, Bob Colacello, who selected all the photographs in addition to writing and editing articles, saw himself as art director, and, in any case, Glenn O'Brien took that title for himself. They made choices they knew would please Andy, yet never dictated what typefaces I could use or prohibited me from using my then-favorite two, Broadway and Busorama—which in retrospect was a big mistake.

I still cannot understand why Andy didn't vet my typography. Before becoming America's pioneering pop artist, he was an accomplished graphic designer and illustrator with a distinctive hand-lettering style. He should have been the first to realize that my pairing of the art deco Broadway type for the nameplate *"Interview"* with the curvaceous Busorama typeface for the subtitle *"Andy Warhol's Film Magazine"* was one of the dumbest combinations ever. It was unsuitably retro and inappropriate; moreover, the two faces lacked any harmony whatsoever. Add to that the heavy Oxford rules I placed at the top and bottom of each page—well, if I were in charge, I would have fired me. Still, no one uttered a displeased peep, and the magazine kept my logo for six issues, even after I voluntarily left for greener pastures (at *Screw*).

Mercifully for readers and staff, with Volume 2, Number 10 the editors brought in a new designer and art director. Soon after I left, *Interview* became a herald of late twentieth-century celebrity, glitz, and fashion, as well as a significant outlet for photography and graphic design. It is so iconic that in 2004 Steidl published an ambitious limited-edition, seven-volume collection, *Andy Warhol's Interview: Volume One.* This mammoth boxed set covered only the publication's first decade, from 1969 to 1979.

Interview evolved into "the definitive guide to the most significant stars of today and tomorrow," say the reprint's editors, Sandra J. Brant and Ingrid Sischy. It was the first magazine to employ a unique question-and-answer format to delve candidly into the minds of celebrities, artists, politicians, filmmakers, musicians, and literary figures. In many of its issues, celebrities interview other celebrities, which was a Warholian conceit that gave *Interview* such deliciously voyeuristic appeal. Yet it is the publication's visual persona—beginning with the haphazard original design, followed by the pseudo–art deco redesign that I perpetrated, and ultimately the introduction of mannered, photo-illustration, celebrity portrait covers by Richard Bernstein—that defined *Interview*'s graphic personality during the disco decade.

Indeed, Bernstein's work marked a unique approach to editorial cover design. His covers owed much to sixties fashion illustration; his photographs heavily retouched with paint, pencil, and pastel monumentalized subjects like nothing else in print. He exaggerated their already glamorous visages through colorful graphic enhancements that made each personality into a veritable mask that hid blemishes while accentuating its auras. He made superstars into megastars. (*Megastar* was also the title of his book of collected *Interview* covers.) His fifteen minutes of fame became weeks, months, and years.

The most memorable *Interview* issue that I worked on (Volume 2, Number 4) was devoted to Luchino Visconti's film *Death in Venice* and was filled with stunning film stills of Dirk Bogarde, Silvana Mangano, and Björn Andrésen. It was a startling issue, one of the last *Interview* to use "handout" or publicity photos. *Interview* gradually shifted from stock to its own photo sessions with the eminences of celebrity and fashion photography—Robert Mapplethorpe, Barry McKinley, Francesco Scavullo, Herb Ritts, Ara Gallant, Peter Beard, Bruce Weber, and Berry Berenson. These and others were given the freedom to create original work. Despite *Interview*'s continued use of yellowing newsprint, these photographs jumped off the pages.

Typographically, the first decade of *Interview* was staid compared to, say, Fred Woodward's *Rolling Stone* of the same period, which expressed its typographic exuberance in so many ways. *Interview*'s interior format was fairly neutral, allowing the photographs to take center stage. It wasn't until the nineties—when Fabien Baron and, later, Tibor Kalman grabbed its design reins—that the magazine's graphic attributes formed a dynamic fusion far exceeding my brief underwhelming contribution. *Interview* went from underground to fashionable, which is the essence of cultural evolution. I could never have been fashionable.

Interview: Andy Warhol's Film Magazine, cover, August 1971 (my last issue).
Art director: Glenn O'Brien. Designer: Steven Heller.

CHAPTER 14

I Am cNot a Punk

B y 1973 the counterculture was experiencing a transformative fizzling
out. My fellows were aging, and a new generation (only a few years
or months younger) of rebellions began to simmer. I was not certain that I would make the cut.

Before Hilly "father of punk" Kristal opened the legendary CBGB
& OMFUG (Country, Bluegrass, Blues & Other Music for Uplifting
Gormandizers) on New York's sleazy Bowery (which has since been gentri-
fied beyond recognition), he was an entrepreneur in other musical realms.
He managed the Village Vanguard, cofounded the Rheingold Central Park
Music Festival, and ran a jazz bar on West 9th Street. Then he opened
Hilly's (a neighborhood bar on West 13th Street) and Hilly's on the Bowery
(both bars failed). I had the opportunity to know Hilly without a clue that
his contribution would be so monumental.

Hilly's on 13th Street (west of Sixth Avenue) was my "Cheers" when
I was in my early twenties. There was no live music (that I can recall), a
limited food menu, a couple of great bartenders, waitresses (including
one who became my girlfriend until she moved to California), and lots of
my friends who worked on underground newspapers. The headquarters

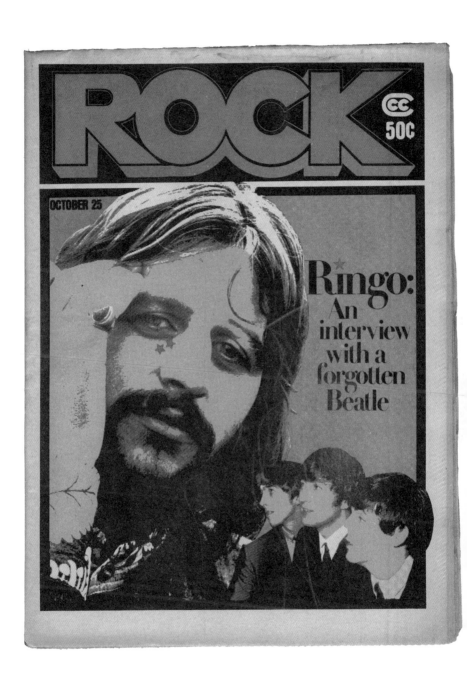

Rock, cover, October 25, 1971. With a Stat King photostat machine I could transform quotidian photographs into artful compositions. Art director: Steven Heller.

Rock, cover, May 10, 1971. The PhotoTypositor allowed for very fluid settings, providing the chance to work more creatively with typography. Art director: Steven Heller.

Rock, cover, June 7, 1971. Rock was notable for the its use of flat Pantone colors that made the images sing. Art director: Steven Heller.

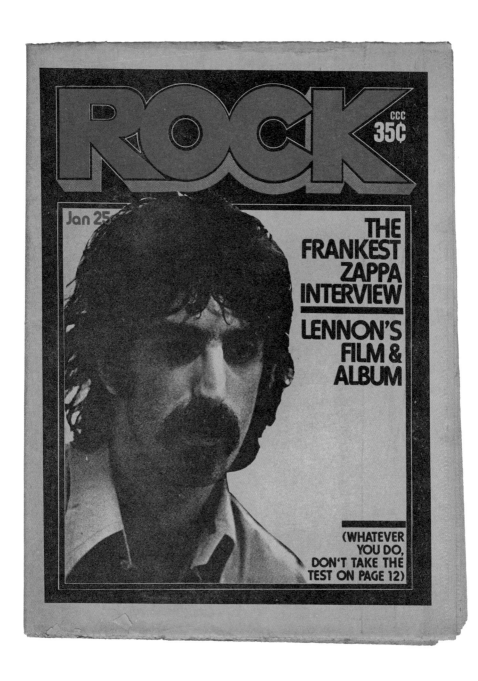

ROCK

CCC
35¢

Jan 25

THE FRANKEST ZAPPA INTERVIEW

LENNON'S FILM & ALBUM

(WHATEVER YOU DO, DON'T TAKE THE TEST ON PAGE 12)

Rock, cover, January 25, 1971. I developed a formulaic format that was indeed different from the mass of other music tabloids published during the time. Art director: Steven Heller.

Rock, cover, July 5, 1971, promoting Grand Funk Railroad with my pitiful interpretation of hard-rock lettering. Art director: Steven Heller.

(Above) *Rook*, April 1971, was a *Rock* self-parody designed for April Fools' Day that suggested a reunion of the Beatles. Fate had other things in store. Art director: Steven Heller. (Opposite) *Rock* interior page for a cover story on the Beatles, January 1971. Running a Beatles story generated a spike in readership. Art director: Steven Heller.

BEATLES
ALONE TOGETHER
or
IS THE WHOLE EVER GREATER THAN THE SUM OF ITS PARTS?

BY STEVEN REINER

Above all else, the Beatles have always charged us with a sense of expectancy. The merit of one work was largely contained in the promise it held for the next. If there was a pitfall it was forgiven as a momentary aberration, for surely it meant something special would soon follow. And, if the music struck a nerve of longing or immediate need, as it so often did, we took it as a piece in an incomplete puzzle, whose solution would answer some great riddle or tell some great tale.

There are no more pieces left for the puzzle now because the Beatles have broken up. Tired of the roles they have been forced to play, they have closed a book in many of our lives and attempted to open new ones for their own. But even with this development, our expectancy, not surprisingly, remains and grows. Now each of the Beatles has released an individually conceived work that indicates the musical and personal directions he has decided to follow, and while these directions are quite dissimilar, they remain rooted in a common past, draw strength from that past, and grow weak away from it. At this point, the Beatles, without each other, are incomplete.

Ringo Starr, *Beaucoups of Blues*

Beaucoups of Blues is Ringo's second solo album. His first, *Sentimental*

Journey, was a high camp escapade down Hollywood Boulevard, with the best of the schmaltzy string studio musicians and arrangers. In *Beaucoups of Blues*, though, Ringo has tempered his comic potential and turned Liverpool charm into effective country song stylization. Ringo is able to attract the best musicians to him, no matter what he wants to sing. Here, with Nashville's finest and help from producer Peter Drake, Ringo's saddened nasal tones croon out country ballads in inventive and stirring new ways. Through most of the songs, Ringo plays himself—the loner and the outcast who bungles his way through his life and loves.

Away from the Beatles Ringo has prospered and grown. Never a great drummer, he has been consistently improving, and it is no accident nor purely a matter of sentimentality that both John and George used Ringo on drums while recording their albums. Ringo carries with him a feeling of nostalgia, of hope and warmth. He is more of a showman than anyone might have imagined while he was hidden behind those drums. While he neither challenges nor confounds us, he is captivating in the independent role he has chosen for himself.

One of the more poignant scenes in "Let it Be" was George's attempt to help Ringo in writing "Octopus's Garden," as Ringo, like a schoolboy

MOUNTAIN

PLAYING BELLY ★ TO BELLY ★ WITH MY MAN BY STEVEN REINER

Rock interior page for a cover story on Leslie West's band Mountain, April 1971. The tabloid page was perfect for playing with big type. Art director: Steven Heller.

B.B. KING

BY DAVID REITMAN

Rock interior page for a story on B. B. King, June 1971. One of my favorite typographic pieces, although I see parts that I could refine. Art director: Steven Heller.

of *Screw* and the *New York Review of Sex & Politics* were right around the corner on 14th Street, and the *East Village Other* was in a loft on East 12th Street.

A few of my friends from *EVO* decided that, since we hung out at Hilly's so often, we would pay him back for his hospitality by producing *Hilly's Gazette*. Playwright Lynda Crawford and writer Dean Latimer edited and wrote the stories under pseudonyms (Lynda was "Lucy Lushful"), a few anonymous folks contributed illustrations and strips,

Rock interior page, December 1970, At *Rock*, I enjoyed working with bold, exaggerated custom lettering that I would combine with high-contrast images. This heading was hand-drawn; the dropped-out body text was a mistake. Art director: Steven Heller.

and I typeset the copy and made the layouts. There was possibly only one issue—at least only one I've found. And amid all the Kristal-CBGB lore, this minor part of his professional life has been forgotten.

Hilly closed his 13th Street bar so he could open his Bowery venue. He invited us all down to the CBGB space, presuming we'd all start hanging out there. "No way," I told him after checking out the bathroom, "this is a disgusting dump!" So much for my talent for predicting New York's hot spots and future historical monuments. Thanks to the above-mentioned gentrification, the building that CBGB once occupied is now a high-priced clothing boutique, but it's nonetheless an NYC landmark.

Before Hilly made punk music history, I was art director of the pre-punk *Rock* magazine. I briefly worked there with Patti Smith, who was destined to be one of CBGB's top acts. She was an associate editor and staff writer and an unknown rock groupie, who let it slip only on one occasion that she knew the playwright Sam Shepard. She'd drop Todd Rundgren's name often, and repeatedly talked about how much she wanted to meet Bob Dylan, but never spoke at all about her lover, the photographer Robert Mapplethorpe. This relationship was the core of her 2010 memoir, *Just Friends*, which does not mention a word about her *Rock* interlude—or me, for that matter.

During her stint at *Rock*, Patti wrote a few stories about her love of 45 rpm records and her interest in musician brothers who were also rock 'n' rollers, "He Ain't Heavy, He's My Brother." Her articles were more poetry than reportage, but each story revealed real passion for her rock obsession.

She met her longtime collaborator, guitarist Lenny Kaye, another accomplished *Rock* writer, at our offices on Seventh Avenue near 14th Street, blocks south from her loft next to the Chelsea Hotel on 23rd Street. I had no idea at the time that she and Lenny were putting together a band to play at an experimental performance space—the Knitting Factory, no less. This ended up becoming a lifetime musical partnership.

Patti and I hung out from time to time, and I was convinced she was bound for nowhere. In fact, after writing for Rock for only a few issues (around two months), she was fired by the music promoter editor who

Patti Smith worked as a writer for *Rock* for two or three months. I did this interior layout, December 1970, for one of her stories on brothers who were also rock musicians. Art director: Steven Heller.

wanted less ethereal reporting and more hard-nosed text. I didn't see or hear about Patti again until three or four years later, when she emerged as the punk-era rock star she always dreamed of becoming. I would never have guessed it possible.

CHAPTER 15

My Times

I n 1973, around the time Hilly planned on closing Hilly's bar and opening CBGB-OMFUG, I was already considering leaving *Screw* and the
underground world I was inhabiting. The taste I had for the punk scene
further convinced me that I had to move on to something more ele-
vated. But I had a social network challenge. While comfortable with my
cohort of cartoonists, illustrators, and writers, I had always "wallowed,"
as my shrink liked to say, in the "mire of social paralysis." His cure, in lieu
of a prescription for antidepressants: "You should drink [booze] more
often; it will loosen you up. Make it easier for you and better for others in
your social group to be around you." He also suggested that group therapy
would help.

I accepted his prescription. However, since I hated the taste of most
alcohol, my fallback drink was rye and ginger ale, the only thing I could
stomach without getting sick. It was my father's preferred cocktail, and
I found the taste was more than tolerable; it was indeed an elixir for
loosening me up. This, in turn, enabled me to be much less anxious about
going to bars, clubs, and social functions in general. Rye and ginger made
me a regular at Hilly's and less directly—but no less significantly—gave

Lisbon's Shrinking Nest Egg

By C. L. Sulzberger

LISBON — Portugal's revolution, whose ultimate course remains unclear, was historically both prompted and financed by the right-wing, army-supported dictatorship created by Antonio de Oliveira Salazar. The revolution has so far succeeded only in creating a left-wing military dictatorship.

...

FOREIGN AFFAIRS

...

The Poppy Whose Sap Is Anti-Life

By Charles B. Rangel

WASHINGTON — The deadly red opium poppies of Turkey are again in full bloom—legally.

When the Turkish Government announced its unilateral decision to lift the ban on opium-poppy cultivation, in violation of executive agreements, it gave repeated assurances that it would act to prevent illegal diversion of opium gum, the raw material for heroin. But now the poppies are being harvested without any evidence that adequate controls have been imposed. Pious promises are not sufficient to block the flow of Turkey's drugs into the United States.

...

Drugs Whose Flowers Are Life

By Stephen L. DeFelice

To all our other troubles, add one more—a crisis in the discovery of valuable and needed new drugs.

Drugs are by far the most effective weapons in the treatment of patients. Imagine life today without polio vaccine, penicillin, digitalis, insulin, diuretics, anesthetics, tranquilizers and all the other drugs that keep us alive and free of pain.

...

Stephen L. DeFelice, M.D., a drug expert and former chief of clinical pharmacology at Walter Reed Army Institute of Research, is the author of "Drug Discovery: The Pending Crisis."

Separating American Messages

By Frank Stanton

The Commission on the Organization of the Government for the Conduct of Foreign Policy, appointed by the Congress and the President, issued its report on July 1. Among its major recommendations, a section on the American overseas informational and cultural programs endorses the findings of an independent nongovernment panel.

...

Frank Stanton served as chairman of the Panel on International Information, Education and Cultural Relations, Center for Strategic and International Studies, Georgetown University. He was formerly president of CBS, Inc.

211

New York Times Op-Ed page, November 2, 1974. This was the very
first page I did for the *Times*, before starting my full-time position there.
Art director: Steven Heller.

212

me the confidence to attend a certain party at Brad Holland's Greene Street loft that triggered the beginning of the most life-changing period of my life to date.

Brad was not a frequent party-giver, but his girlfriend, Emily, had the hostess gene. Many of their guests included my existing friends, and a few of them—illustrators, designers, and art directors from *EVO*, the *New York Ace*, *Screw*, *High Times*, and other periodicals—had already begun to dig themselves out of their underground caves for jobs and assignments in aboveground media. My best friend at the time, Ray Schultz—an exceptional writer who fashioned his witty, sarcastic, NYC-streetwise writing style on Jimmy Breslin and Pete Hamill—had already published his first big article in the *New York Times Magazine*. P. J. O'Rourke, who was writing satire for the *New York Ace*, was destined to become editor of the *National Lampoon*. And many of the artists I hired to draw *Screw* covers had joined J. C. Suares's stable of *Times* Op-Ed illustrators. I was envious, and I hungrily looked for a connection into that world. I had no idea the connection would begin that night.

I had never met Ruth Ansel before the party. In fact, I am not certain I even knew her name or that she was art director of the *New York Times Magazine*, which was the award-winning-design flagship of the newspaper. Her elegance seemed out of place in Brad's SoHo loft. But Brad had done some work for her and made a demonstrative point of introducing us. I'm pretty certain he told her I was art director of *Screw*. This was not always a door opener, especially with women, but it was best to get it out in the open. I was in enough of a rye-and-ginger-ale zone (and it didn't take much to get there) to feel comfortable having an easygoing conversation with Ruth. We talked about magazine stuff, and I suggested we have a lunch meeting where I could show her my portfolio. "I was looking for something less underground," I told her.

I squeezed a lot more examples than from *Screw* into my oversized leather carrying case, but the *Screw* pages and spreads included what I considered my best type layouts. Minus the porno, they were the closest things to what Ruth did with the *Magazine*. In a foolish effort to disguise the content, I made 60-percent reductions of the tamer spreads and pages, while showing the best covers full size.

The meeting went better than I could have expected. We talked about mutual acquaintances and magazines we liked and didn't. She told me about her time as co-art director of *Harper's Bazaar,* where she worked with legendary photographers such as Richard Avedon and Hiro and employed fine artists, including Andy Warhol. To top it off, she genuinely liked my examples and suggested that I come work for her for a trial period. She asked to hold onto the portfolio so she could show it to Louis Silverstein, the *Times* corporate art director responsible for the famous "I Got My Job through the New York Times" subway posters.

Lou wielded a lot of power because he knew how to navigate through the *Times* corporate side and the daily and Sunday *Times* editorial departments. Although the editorial, letters, and Op-Ed pages were independent of the news and Sunday departments, he designed the first Op-Ed pages and instituted the Op-Ed illustration style, which rejected typically captioned editorial cartoons (like Herblock's cartoons in the *Washington Post*) for drawings that were more artfully metaphoric or symbolic and complemented the stories. In other words, the illustrations were more independent than the slavishly literal kind found in most magazines. This style spilled over into other newly designed Sunday sections of the *Times* as well.

Lou made a smart decision to hire J. C. Suares as art director of the Op-Ed page. J. C. was a keen connoisseur of European and American satirical and political art, and he instinctively knew who to hire to expand on Lou's vision. The problem was, they did not get along.

A week or two after leaving my portfolio with Ruth, she called to tell me that Lou had another job in mind for me. She made him promise that I could work on the *Magazine* for at least one spread an issue. He agreed. An appointment was made for me to meet him, and I was offered the Op-Ed position, sort of.

"I'd like you to help with the Op-Ed," Lou said noncommittally.

"Does that mean 'help' as in art director?" I asked, hoping for a definitive response.

"Sure. Yes, of course," he said, in what I came to learn was his quirky way of navigating *Times* politics. He rattled off an annual salary that was less than I was earning at *Screw,* but I didn't care.

There was a slight problem, though. Lou was only nominally in charge of the Op-Ed art department. Lou had tried to fire J. C. in the past, but he was protected by founding editor Harrison Salisbury and his deputy David Schneiderman, until J. C. stepped over one line too far by organizing an

Op-Ed exhibit at the Louvre without obtaining the *Times* corporate consent. The exhibit was a great accomplishment, but J. C. was arrogant in the way he handled it. Lou found the grounds needed for termination. J. C. was not aware that I was selected to be his heir apparent. Prior to me a few art directors (including Seymour Chwast) were given tryouts, and another art director had been appointed and then pushed aside. Although I don't think J. C. would have put my name forward for the job, he jumped on board when he could and, technically speaking, gave his blessing.

The Op-Ed job was another improbable dream made real. It was also a nightmare. There was the J. C. legacy to contend with. Some of his artists were heroes to me, and I was overjoyed to work with André François, Ronald Searle, Edward Gorey, Ralph Steadman, TIM, and many more. And I worked with my old friends—Brad Holland, Marshall Arisman, Philippe Weisbecker, and Sue Coe—who were regular contributors. But I was also saddled with some otherwise solid Op-Ed people whose work I disliked: Eugene Mihaesco was among the stalwarts and a J. C. ally. And then there was J. C. himself. I resented having to accept whatever he submitted and that a lot of it looked like it was copied from Saul Steinberg. (Mihaesco was even more blatant.) I once called Saul to ask him if he'd work for the Op-Ed. "No!" he blurted, "You've already got Mihaesco."

To make my own signature on the page, I had two strategies. In addition to hiring veteran and untested illustrators (most of the latter would visit my office with their portfolios), I'd make weekly visits to galleries around New York to look for talent. And I would encourage artists like Claes Oldenburg, Marvin Israel, Mary Frank, and H. C. Westermann to contribute work they'd done already.

I also played around with the design of the Op-Ed page. For my favorite layout, devoted to the Kennedy assassination, I enlarged a photo of the murder weapon (a Mannlicher-Carcano rifle) to fill the page from top to bottom and leaned it against a column of type. David Schneiderman, who was off that day, told me if he had been in the office, he wouldn't have allowed me to do it.

David was not always as disagreeable as it sounds. However, the editor who replaced Harrison Salisbury, Charlotte Curtis, was my nemesis. We did not get along, and letters she sent to Lou prove it. For my part, she was visually ignorant in the worst way: she didn't acknowledge what she did not know. I knew my tenure on the Op-Ed was hanging on by a string when she

The Truth Is Needed

By Tom Wicker

IN THE NATION

Carol in a Time of Nontente

By Wallace Carroll

Excursion Into Maudlin

By Russell Baker

OBSERVER

South Bronx Is Burning

By James P. Brown

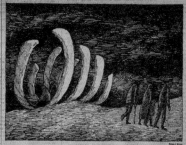

Christmas, 1974

By May Sarton

May Sarton, a poet and novelist, is author of "Journal of a Solitude."

New York Times Op-Ed page, December 24, 1974. Christmas Eve was the perfect day to publish this slightly dour illustration by the master of macabre, Edward Gorey. Art director: Steven Heller.

They Aren't Dimes That Boy's Handing Out

By Russell Baker

Napoleon's Patch on Uncle Sam's Breeches

By Edward A. Morse

Looking Into An Aegean Crystal Ball

By C. L. Sulzberger

OBSERVER

FOREIGN AFFAIRS

Yugoslavia: Behind the Revelry, Retreat

By Mihajlo Mihajlov

New York Times Op-Ed page, October 12, 1974. This was a Saturday page, and Saturdays rarely contained the advertisements that took up a quarter of the art and text space on other days of the week. Illustrator: Marshall Arisman. Art director: Steven Heller.

217

Unwelcome News for Mr. Ford

By Tom Wicker

The Men Who Are Not Running for President

WASHINGTON
By James Reston

The Old Red Marxillac— She Ain't What She Used to Be

By Bryan Magee

The Politics of the Panama Postponement

FOREIGN AFFAIRS
By C. L. Sulzberger

New York Times Op-Ed page, November 9, 1975. James Grashow,
who made intricate wood engravings, was one of my proudest discoveries.
Or maybe he discovered me. Art director: Steven Heller.

Thanks-Giving —1974

WASHINGTON

By James Reston

The No-Holes-in-the-Shoes Blues

By Hans Rosenhaupt

Mondale And Udall

IN THE NATION

By Tom Wicker

For Equal, Dual Sovereignty in Jerusalem

By Lord Caradon

Neither Garbage Nor 'Salad Baskets'

By C. L. Sulzberger

FOREIGN AFFAIRS

New York Times Op-Ed page, November 24, 1974. Every Saturday I would hunt for artists at New York galleries and pulled in quite good artists that way. One of them was H. C. Westermann, whose wooden box was a complement for this story. Art director: Steven Heller.

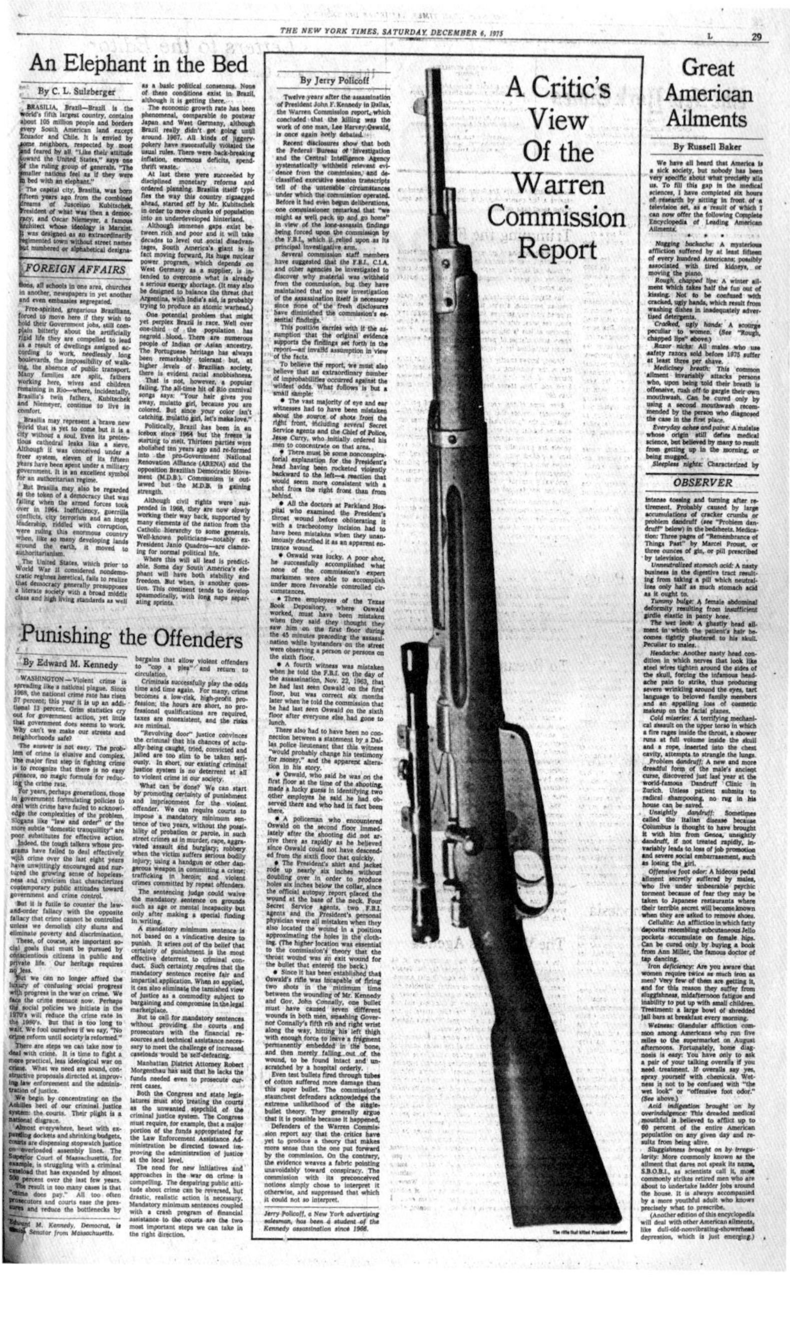

An Elephant in the Bed

By C. L. Sulzberger

FOREIGN AFFAIRS

Punishing the Offenders

By Edward M. Kennedy

A Critic's View Of the Warren Commission Report

By Jerry Policoff

Great American Ailments

By Russell Baker

OBSERVER

New York Times Op-Ed page, December 6, 1975. One of my favorite pages involved leaning the rifle that was used to kill President John F. Kennedy against a full column of type. Art director: Steven Heller.

said something minor yet insulting enough to me that I lunged at her and almost grabbed her neck. I was held back by David and told to calm down. Arrogant though she was, Charlotte knew she had stepped over the line. She apologized, but things were tense enough after that. I remained at the Op-Ed only a couple weeks longer.

One of the valid complaints Charlotte had was that I was spending too much time at my concurrent *Times* position as art director of the *Book Review*. I went on to spend almost thirty years there under six different editors. Some were great in that they gave me room to try things; some difficult in that they did not. Yet it was the job that opened the most doors for me and was the foundation of my professional life as an art director and all that followed. But that's another story.

ACKNOWLEDGMENTS

My sincere thanks to Jennifer Thompson, my editor at Princeton Architectural Press, for her support, advice, and enthusiasm. And to Clare Jacobson, copy editor, and Paul Wagner, design director.

Gratitude goes to Tom Bodkin, Gail Anderson, Veronique Vienne, and Eric Himmel for reading and critiquing different iterations of the manuscript.

My gratitude to Louise Fili and Matt Smith at Louise Fili Ltd for their contributions to the book and cover design. And to Beth Kleber for helping me locate some of the rare visual material in the SVA Milton Glaser Study Center Archive.

There were many people who influenced me during the years covered herein whom I have not referenced by name. I've had the good fortune to know some wonderful colleagues and collaborators in my formative years. Predictably, I've learned a little something from each experience with them. Thanks to all.

I have not mentioned friends and acquaintances who certainly would have made the cut if I had stretched the time span of this book further into my Times and School of Visual Arts years. So, here's a tip of the hat to a few of those individuals who have made such positive impressions on my life: Seymour Chwast, Paul Rand, Milton Glaser, Sarah Jane Freymann, Mirko Ilic, Paula Scher, Debbie Millman, David Rhodes, Lita Talarico.

Finally, thanks to those readers of *The Daily Heller*, who repeatedly have asked me to write a memoir. I appreciate your interest and support.